Selfless LIVING IN A Selfie WORLD

by

pam gillaspie

Dedicated to . . .

Sue and Dave Olson, my Mom and Dad, who have modeled selfless living every single day of my life.

Acknowledgements

It's easy for readers to think that a book only belongs to the author whose name appears on the cover. Nothing could be further from the truth. Thanks as always to Rick Purdy and Pete DeLacy for walking through multiple drafts with me from a theological and editorial standpoint. Thanks to Jan Silvious whose influence prompted my thinking toward the topic. Thanks to Kay Arthur for the critical Uzziah-Isaiah connection that I hadn't seen on my own. Thanks to my husband, Dave, for the cover and interior design of the book. Thanks to the marketing and design department of Scott Rimell, Scott Grizzle, John Phillips, and Brian Woodlief into whose hands the project goes when it leaves mine.
Above all, glory to God who allows us to join in His work in this world!

Scripture taken from the
NEW AMERICAN STANDARD BIBLE®,
© Copyright 1960, 1962, 1963, 1968,
1971, 1972, 1973, 1975, 1977, 1995
by The Lockman Foundation.
Used by permission. (www.Lockman.org)

Scripture quotations marked (ESV) are
from The Holy Bible, English Standard
Version® (ESV®), copyright © 2001 by
Crossway, a publishing ministry of Good
News Publishers. Used by permission. All
rights reserved.

Precept, Precept Ministries International,
Precept Ministries International the
Inductive Bible Study People, the Plumb
Bob design, Precept Upon Precept and
Sweeter than Chocolate are trademarks of
Precept Ministries International.

Copyright © 2015 by Pam Gillaspie
Published by Precept Ministries
International
P.O. Box 182218
Chattanooga, Tennessee 37422
www.precept.org

ISBN 978-1-62119-421-7

Selfless LIVING IN A Selfie WORLD

There is nothing quite like your favorite pair of jeans. You can dress them up, you can dress them down. You can work in them, play in them, shop in them . . . live in them. They always feel right. It is my hope that the structure of this Bible study will fit you like those jeans; that it will work with your life right now, right where you are whether you're new to this whole Bible thing or whether you've been studying the Book for years!

How is this even be possible? Smoke and mirrors, perhaps? The new mercilessly thrown in the deep end? The experienced given pompoms and the job of simply cheering others on? None of the above.

Flexible inductive Bible studies are designed with options that will allow you to go as deep each week as you desire. If you're just starting out and feeling a little overwhelmed, stick with the main text and don't think a second thought about the sidebar assignments. If you're looking for a challenge, then take the sidebar prompts and go ahead and dig all the way to China! As you move along through the study, think of the sidebars and "Digging Deeper" boxes as that 2% of lycra that you find in certain jeans . . . the wiggle-room that will help them fit just right.

Beginners may find that they want to start adding in some of the optional assignments as they go along. Experts may find that when three children are throwing up for three days straight, foregoing those assignments for the week is the way to live wisely.

Life has a way of ebbing and flowing and this study is designed to ebb and flow right along with it!

Enjoy!

Contents

How to use this study

Flexible inductive Bible studies meet you where you are and take you as far as you want to go.

1. WEEKLY STUDY: The main text guides you through the complete topic of study for the week.

2. FYI boxes: For Your Information boxes provide bite-sized material to shed additional light on the topic.

> ## FYI:
> **Reading Tip: Begin with prayer**
> You may have heard this a million times over and if this is a million and one, so be it. Whenever you read or study God's Word, first pray and ask His Spirit to be your Guide.

3. ONE STEP FURTHER and other sidebar boxes: Sidebar boxes give you the option to push yourself a little further. If you have extra time or are looking for an extra challenge, you can try one, all, or any number in between! These boxes give you the ultimate in flexibility.

> ## ONE STEP FURTHER:
> **Word Study: *torah*/law**
> The first of eight Hebrew key words we encounter for God's Word is *torah* translated "law." If you're up for a challenge this week, do a word study to learn what you can about *torah*. Run a concordance search and examine where the word *torah* appears in the Old Testament and see what you can learn from the contexts.
> If you decide to look for the word for "law" in the New Testament, you'll find that the primary Greek word is *nomos*.
> Be sure to see what Paul says about the law in Galatians 3 and what Jesus says in Matthew 5.

4. DIGGING DEEPER boxes: If you're looking to go further, Digging Deeper sections will help you sharpen your skills as you continue to mine the truths of Scripture for yourself.

> ## Digging Deeper
> **What else does God's Word say about counselors?**
> If you can, spend some time this week digging around for what God's Word says about counselors.
>
> Start by considering what you already know about counsel from the Word of God and see if you can actually show where these truths are in the Bible. Make sure that the Word actually says what you think it says.

Week One
Mirror, Mirror on the Wall . . .

"He must increase, but I must decrease."
–John the Baptist, John 3:30

We live in a culture that venerates pride, self-sufficiency, and getting ahead above just about everything else. Pursuing humility seems weak, servile, and to bottom-line folks perhaps bordering on stupidity. God's Word and the testimony of those who obey it tell an entirely different story, one upside down from the cultural narrative that continuously turns the camera toward self.

God's ways are not man's ways; they are profoundly better. We know this, but still we're lured by a "selfie" culture that says "Live big because you are the center of the universe!" to every person who breathes on the planet. But let me ask you one question: *How do you like hanging out with people who think and behave like everything revolves around them?* My guess is that you don't like it any better than I do.

Let me follow up with one more question: *Do you know what one of the main criticisms leveled against the Church is today?* It's self-importance, just another way of saying arrogance.*

While it isn't surprising that the Bible makes a huge case for humility before a Sovereign Creator, it's hard to miss the paradox that our selfie culture both breeds and feeds arrogance, but at the same time hates it . . . especially arrogance in the Church.

Arrogance has a stench about it that offends both people and God Himself. Humility, though, has a fragrance; a sweet aroma noticed by men and pleasing to God.

FYI:

If You're in a Class
Complete **Week One** together on your first day of class. This will be a great way to start getting to know one another and will help those who are newer to Bible study get their bearings.

*David Kinnaman and Gabe Lyons, *unChristian: What a New Generation Thinks About Christianity—and Why it Matters.* Grand Rapids, MI: Baker Books, 2007, p. 26.

CONSIDER the WAY you THINK

Consider for a moment what kind of scent lingers about your life today. Is it sweet and fragrant, pleasing to all who come near . . . or is it indicating something's amiss?

What "smells" right in your life today? Explain.

What "smells" wrong? Explain.

How do you view humility? Do you see it as virtuous or weak? Explain. Does false humility ever play into your thinking, planning, and actions? Give some examples.

How do you view arrogance? Do you distinguish between pride and arrogance? If so, how?

Do you struggle with pride? Are you annoyed when you see it in others? Explain.

While the Bible is packed with men and women who exemplify humility, none did so more thoroughly or clearly than John the Baptist. Jesus Himself commends him to the disciples when He says " . . . among those born of women there is no one greater than John . . ." immediately making him a person of interest. We follow Jesus first and foremost, but we can learn to do that better by paying attention to the lives of others who followed well.

FYI:

Suggested Reading . . .

unChristian: What a New Generation Thinks About Christianity . . . and Why it Matters by David Kinnaman and Gabe Lyons.

In this critical but disturbing book, Kinnaman, President of the Barna Group, and Lyons investigate how a new generation views Christianity. Think humility is only important to God? When you read this book, you'll think again.

FYI:

Start with Prayer

You've probably heard it before and if we study together in the future, you're sure to hear it again. Whenever you read or study God's Word, first pray and ask the Lord to guide you with His Holy Spirit. Jesus says that the Spirit will lead us into all truth.

JOHN THE BAPTIST

SETTING the SCENE

This text immediately follows the Apostle John's recap of Jesus' conversation with Nicodemus. The Pharisee had come to talk to Jesus under the cover of night—likely to maintain secrecy—because he recognized mere man could not perform the signs Jesus had. Jesus quickly turned the conversation to the need for a person to be born again to see the kingdom of God.

OBSERVE the TEXT of SCRIPTURE

READ John 3:22-36 and **MARK** references to *Jesus* and *John the Baptist*.

John 3:22-36

22 *After these things Jesus and His disciples came into the land of Judea, and there He was spending time with them and baptizing.*

23 *John also was baptizing in Aenon near Salim, because there was much water there; and* people *were coming and were being baptized—*

24 *for John had not yet been thrown into prison.*

25 *Therefore there arose a discussion on the part of John's disciples with a Jew about purification.*

26 *And they came to John and said to him, "Rabbi, He who was with you beyond the Jordan, to whom you have testified, behold, He is baptizing and all are coming to Him."*

27 *John answered and said, "A man can receive nothing unless it has been given him from heaven.*

28 *"You yourselves are my witnesses that I said, 'I am not the Christ,' but, 'I have been sent ahead of Him.'*

29 *"He who has the bride is the bridegroom; but the friend of the bridegroom, who stands and hears him, rejoices greatly because of the bridegroom's voice. So this joy of mine has been made full.*

30 *"He must increase, but I must decrease.*

31 *"He who comes from above is above all, he who is of the earth is from the earth and speaks of the earth. He who comes from heaven is above all.*

32 *"What He has seen and heard, of that He testifies; and no one receives His testimony.*

33 *"He who has received His testimony has set his seal to* this, *that God is true.*

34 *"For He whom God has sent speaks the words of God; for He gives the Spirit without measure.*

35 *"The Father loves the Son and has given all things into His hand.*

36 *"He who believes in the Son has eternal life; but he who does not obey the Son will not see life, but the wrath of God abides on him."*

FYI:

Camel Hair and a Belt
Have you ever considered how much what we wear influences self-centeredness or at least self-focus? Advertisers peddle clothes modeled on Photoshopped beauties to people who want to look good for others . . . and we haven't mentioned accessories yet! John had one outfit—a garment of camel's hair—and one necessary accessory—a leather belt.

He wasted no time on "What do I wear today?", no emotional energy on "What will they think of my outfit?", and no resources on things he didn't need.

DISCUSS with your GROUP or PONDER on your own . . .

What happens to John's ministry when Jesus comes on the scene?

ONE STEP FURTHER:

Thinking for Yourself

If you have a working knowledge of the Bible and a little time on your hands, think of individuals in the Bible whose lives shed light on humility and pride. Jot down your thoughts below. Sure, the study is going to bring up names, but why be dependent on workbook questions? Think for yourself. Anticipate questions. *You* rightly divide the Word of truth. Record your observations below.

What does John make of this turn of events? Summarize in paragraph or list form how John compares himself to Jesus.

What does John say about God?

How would your life change if you followed John's paradigm "He must increase, but I must decrease"?

Do you ever increase yourself and decrease Jesus in day-to-day life? If so, how?

Do you ever increase yourself and decrease Jesus in ministry? Again, if so, how? What about corporately? Do churches ever elevate individuals or ministries above Jesus? Explain.

What do you notice happening in your life when you seek to increase your position or status? Have you observed times when you are more prone to this type of behavior? If so, when? Why?

What are some biblical ways to counteract this behavior and live John's mindset?

USING AN INDUCTIVE APPROACH

As we study together, we'll use an inductive approach toward the Bible. With increases in connectivity and information technology today, we have access to study tools and resources unparalleled in history, but the main thing remains the main thing—the Bible itself.

Inductive study has three main components that we'll walk through step-by-step: *observation, interpretation,* and *application.*

Observation asks: *What does the text say?*

Interpretation asks: *What does the text mean?*

Application asks: *How can I apply this truth in my life?*

Together they lead to transformation by the Spirit through the Word.

MARKING the text of Scripture is one tool that will help us to observe the text well. We identify key words by reading carefully, then we mark them. As we mark, we ASK the 5W and H questions (*Who? What? When? Where? Why?* and *How?*).

SIZING UP THE LANDSCAPE

Over the next few weeks we'll study God's Word together to find out for ourselves how we can live selfless lives in a selfie world. We'll discover biblical solutions to counteract the clawing and climbing behavior so ingrained into the hearts of fallen people. First, though, let's take a look together at the landscape of the culture we live in and a look at what led us there.

SETTING the SCENE

Writing to his child in the faith, Paul warns Timothy about what the last days will look like. Timothy lived in the last days and so do we.

FYI:

The Last Days are Here

When Paul talks about the last (Greek: *eschatos*) days, he is not referring to some far-off, distant time. He is referring to the age that began with Christ's incarnation. Are we in "the last days"? We absolutely are, as everyone since Jesus' time.

OBSERVE the TEXT of SCRIPTURE

READ 2 Timothy 3:1-5 and **UNDERLINE** characteristics of people in the last days.

2 Timothy 3:1-5

1   But realize this, that in the last days difficult times will come.

2   For men will be lovers of self, lovers of money, boastful, arrogant, revilers, disobedient to parents, ungrateful, unholy,

3   unloving, irreconcilable, malicious gossips, without self-control, brutal, haters of good,

4   treacherous, reckless, conceited, lovers of pleasure rather than lovers of God,

5   holding to a form of godliness, although they have denied its power; Avoid such men as these.

DISCUSS with your GROUP or PONDER on your own . . .

Who is Paul talking about in this section? **What** are the people Paul describes like?

What does Paul tell Timothy to do in verse 1? Why will this matter?

When will these people be around?

Where will they be?

Why are they a concern?

How are these characteristics counter to God and His ways?

Does Paul's description of the last days match what you see in your worlds? Explain.

Who specifically does Paul tell Timothy to avoid? Does he put parameters on it?
Explain.

Are there any people in your life that Paul might tell you to avoid? Why?

SETTING the SCENE

James writes sobering words to fellow believers concerning different kinds of wisdom.

OBSERVE the TEXT of SCRIPTURE

READ James 3:13-18 and **MARK** references to *jealousy* and *selfish ambition*.

James 3:13-18

13 *Who among you is wise and understanding? Let him show by his good behavior his deeds in the gentleness of wisdom.*

14 *But if you have bitter jealousy and selfish ambition in your heart, do not be arrogant and so lie against the truth.*

15 *This wisdom is not that which comes down from above, but is earthly, natural, demonic.*

16 *For where jealousy and selfish ambition exist, there is disorder and every evil thing.*

17 *But the wisdom from above is first pure, then peaceable, gentle, reasonable, full of mercy and good fruits, unwavering, without hypocrisy.*

18 *And the seed whose fruit is righteousness is sown in peace by those who make peace.*

DISCUSS with your GROUP or PONDER on your own . . .

What two wisdoms does James contrast in this section?

Describe earthly wisdom. What characterizes it? What is its source? How does it live? What is its relationship to the truth?

Describe the wisdom from above. What characterizes this wisdom? What is its source? How does it live? What is its relationship to the truth?

Based on what you've seen in the text, do you think you're able to identify these two wisdoms in others? How about in yourself?

Is your life ever marked by "bitter jealousy and selfish ambition"? Explain.

Have you seen people demonstrate the "wisdom from above" that James talks about? If so, how has it affected you? What have you learned from examples you've seen?

THE HEIGHT OF ARROGANCE

There is arrogance and then there is *arrogance*. The final two texts that we are going to look at this week show arrogance in all its puffed up false glory. The arrogance displayed is so great that many scholars tie the texts not only to the height of human pride but to the fall of Satan as well. Regardless of whether these speak of mortal men alone or also of Satan himself, we can learn much about arrogance and its outcome from Ezekiel 28:11-19 and Isaiah 14:12-15.

SETTING the SCENE

In Ezekiel 28, the temporal king in view is the king of Tyre, but much of the descriptive language seems to point to someone else who exhibits the same character traits and behaviors.

ONE STEP FURTHER:

Word Study: Jealousy and Selfish Ambition

If you have some extra time this week, see if you can find the Greek words for "jealousy" and "selfish ambition." Then see where else and how else they are used in the New Testament and record your findings below.

ONE STEP FURTHER:

Ezekiel 28:1-10

If you have extra time this week, add the early verses of Ezekiel 28 to your study and record your observations below. What caused the leader of Tyre's heart to be lifted up? How did he behave because of it? What judgment did God bring?

OBSERVE the TEXT of SCRIPTURE

READ Ezekiel 28:11-19 and **MARK** every reference to the *king of Tyre* including pronouns.

Ezekiel 28:11-19

11 *Again the word of the LORD came to me saying,*

12 *"Son of man, take up a lamentation over the king of Tyre and say to him, 'Thus says the Lord GOD,*

"You had the seal of perfection,

Full of wisdom and perfect in beauty.

13 *"You were in Eden, the garden of God;*

Every precious stone was your covering:

The ruby, the topaz and the diamond;

The beryl, the onyx and the jasper;

The lapis lazuli, the turquoise and the emerald;

And the gold, the workmanship of your settings and sockets,

Was in you.

On the day that you were created

They were prepared.

14 *"You were the anointed cherub who covers,*

And I placed you there.

You were on the holy mountain of God;

You walked in the midst of the stones of fire.

15 *"You were blameless in your ways*

From the day you were created

Until unrighteousness was found in you.

16 *"By the abundance of your trade*

You were internally filled with violence,

And you sinned;

Therefore I have cast you as profane

From the mountain of God.

And I have destroyed you, O covering cherub,

From the midst of the stones of fire.

17 *"Your heart was lifted up because of your beauty;*

You corrupted your wisdom by reason of your splendor.

I cast you to the ground;

I put you before kings,

That they may see you.

18 *"By the multitude of your iniquities,*

   In the unrighteousness of your trade

   You profaned your sanctuaries.

   Therefore I have brought fire from the midst of you;

   It has consumed you,

   And I have turned you to ashes on the earth

   In the eyes of all who see you.

19 *"All who know you among the peoples*

   Are appalled at you;

   You have become terrified

   And you will cease to be forever." ' "

DISCUSS with your GROUP or PONDER on your own . . .

Who is speaking in this section and who is being spoken to?

Who was the lamentation to be pronounced over?

List everything you learned about the king of Tyre based on what you marked in the text.

FYI:

Ezekiel: Writing from Exile
Ezekiel was both a priest and a prophet to the exiles during Judah's captivity in Babylon.

Now, go back and look at your list and mark entries that describe something more than a mortal man. What makes those descriptions different?

Some commentators think this text includes words to the historical king of Tyre but that parts of it seem to go further to describe another one who was like him—Satan when he fell from heaven in the biggest display of self-glorification ever. Regardless of which parts of Ezekiel 28:2-19 are applicable to a human ruler and which to an angelic ruler, we see case studies not only in self-elevation and worship but also in the behaviors these lead to. Let's look closer.

What was the king like in the beginning? What good qualities was he given and noted for?

What happened to his heart?

What did he do to his own wisdom?

What does this tell us about non-revealed wisdom's ability to keep people on the straight and narrow?

What else resulted after the king's heart and wisdom were corrupted?

How did God view his actions? How did He respond?

Notes

How would you describe God's view of His creatures exalting and worshipping themselves?

How does our culture exalt and worship itself?

How do you succumb to this in your life? What are some specific ways believers can live counter-culturally?

ONE STEP FURTHER:

Get the Whole Context

While we're focusing on Isaiah 14:12-15, the context for these verses is Isaiah 13:1–14:23. If you have time this week check out the full context. Remember, context is king in matters of interpretation! When you're done reading, record your observations below.

SETTING the SCENE

In the following verses from Isaiah, the subject is related to "the king of Babylon" in verse 4. Like the Ezekiel text, some think these verses are also a reference to Satan's fall. Even if this is not the case, we see arrogance and rebellion against God fully on display.

OBSERVE the TEXT of SCRIPTURE

READ Isaiah 14:3-15 and **MARK** references to the *star of the morning* including synonyms and pronouns.

Isaiah 14:3-15

3 And it will be in the day when the LORD gives you rest from your pain and turmoil and harsh service in which you have been enslaved,

4 that you will take up this taunt against the king of Babylon, and say,

"How the oppressor has ceased,

And how fury has ceased!

5 "The LORD has broken the staff of the wicked,

The scepter of rulers

6 Which used to strike the peoples in fury with unceasing strokes,

Which subdued the nations in anger with unrestrained persecution.

7 "The whole earth is at rest and is quiet;

They break forth into shouts of joy.

8 "Even the cypress trees rejoice over you, and the cedars of Lebanon, saying,

'Since you were laid low, no tree cutter comes up against us.'

Week One: **Mirror, Mirror on the Wall . . .**

ONE STEP FURTHER:

Star of the Morning

If you have some extra time this week, see what you can discover about the phrase "star of the morning" (Isaiah 14:12). What current name do we derive from it? Record your findings below.

9"Sheol from beneath is excited over you to meet you when you come;

It arouses for you the spirits of the dead, all the leaders of the earth;

It raises all the kings of the nations from their thrones.

10 "They will all respond and say to you,

'Even you have been made weak as we,

You have become like us.

11 'Your pomp and the music of your harps

Have been brought down to Sheol;

Maggots are spread out as your bed beneath you

And worms are your covering.'

12 "How you have fallen from heaven,

O star of the morning, son of the dawn!

You have been cut down to the earth,

You who have weakened the nations!

13 "But you said in your heart,

'I will ascend to heaven;

I will raise my throne above the stars of God,

And I will sit on the mount of assembly

In the recesses of the north.

14 'I will ascend above the heights of the clouds;

I will make myself like the Most High.'

15 "Nevertheless you will be thrust down to Sheol,

To the recesses of the pit."

DISCUSS with your GROUP or PONDER on your own . . .

Who is being addressed in this section? How is he described in verse 12? What has he done? What has happened to him?

What did he say prior to being cut down?

Based on his statements, how does he view himself?

How does he view God?

For the moment, let's assume this is talking about a human king over Babylon. What kind of behavior would you expect from someone with these views of God and himself?

How does a proper view of God impact how we view ourselves?

What's your view of God? What is it based on?

What is your view of yourself in light of your view of God? Is it biblical or not? Explain.

@THE END OF THE DAY . . .

As we finish our lesson this week, spend some time evaluating your life. Which direction do you typically have the camera turned? Are you self- or others-focused? Listen to your conversations. Watch your social media life. Who are they about? Our world in general and certain industries in particular have made self-promotion a god . . . but there is only One God. How are you doing at living in light of this truth?

Week Two
Wrong Perception, Wrong Reality

"In the year that King Uzziah died, I saw the Lord . . . "
– Isaiah 6:1 ESV

Pop psychology tells us that perception is reality but truth, like it or not, exists apart from perception. In other words, my opinion can't change what is true. Your view doesn't alter what *is*. This week we'll contrast two biblical characters whose lives overlapped, one a king, the other a prophet. One perceived himself as bigger than he truly was; the other saw the truth of God and so saw himself in proper perspective. A skewed perspective leads to a bent life.

Notes

REMEMBERING

Take a few minutes to summarize what you learned last week.

INDUCTIVE FOCUS:

What is a Key Word?

A key word or phrase is critical to the message of the passage; in a sense it "unlocks" the meaning of a text. Often, key words will be repeated.

In historical narrative, people or characters are key to understanding the text, so we mark them as key words.

THE KING

OBSERVE the TEXT of SCRIPTURE

READ 2 Kings 15:1-7 and **MARK** every reference to *Azariah* including synonyms and pronouns.

2 Kings 15:1-7

1   In the twenty-seventh year of Jeroboam king of Israel, Azariah son of Amaziah king of Judah became king.

2   He was sixteen years old when he became king, and he reigned fifty-two years in Jerusalem; and his mother's name was Jecoliah of Jerusalem.

3   He did right in the sight of the LORD, according to all that his father Amaziah had done.

4   Only the high places were not taken away; the people still sacrificed and burned incense on the high places.

5   The LORD struck the king, so that he was a leper to the day of his death. And he lived in a separate house, while Jotham the king's son was over the household, judging the people of the land.

6   Now the rest of the acts of Azariah and all that he did, are they not written in the Book of the Chronicles of the Kings of Judah?

7   And Azariah slept with his fathers, and they buried him with his fathers in the city of David, and Jotham his son became king in his place.

DISCUSS with your GROUP or PONDER on your own . . .

Who becomes king of Judah in verse 1? How old is he at the time? How long does he reign?

What kind of a king is he "in the sight of the LORD"? What does he do? What doesn't he do?

What happens to him in verse 5? What effect does it have and how long does it last?

How would you characterize Azariah based on this passage?

What big "Why?" question is left unanswered by this text?

Does the text tell us where to find the answer? Explain.

> **INDUCTIVE FOCUS:**
>
> **Make A List**
>
> Key words serve as the basis for informational lists that also help us to observe the text more carefully.
>
> We've already learned quite a bit about Azariah simply by reading texts that contain references to him and asking 5W and H questions. In order to look a little more closely, let's use our MARKINGs of Azariah to MAKE A LIST of everything the text says about him in 2 Kings 15. As you make your list, don't forget to include the reference. Here are a couple of entries to get you started:
>
> • son of Amaziah (15:1)
>
> • king of Judah (15:1)

SETTING the SCENE

In a parallel account to 1 Kings 15:1-7, the chronicler refers to King Azariah ("Yahweh has helped") as Uzziah ("Yahweh is my strength"). While the names have a very different appearance in English, they vary by only one letter in Hebrew. Some commentators think that Uzziah may have been the king's throne name. Regardless, it is important to know that Azariah and Uzziah are the same person.

OBSERVE the TEXT of SCRIPTURE

READ 2 Chronicles 26:1-23 and **MARK** every reference to *Uzziah* including synonyms and pronouns. Also **MARK** every reference to *God/the LORD*.

2 Chronicles 26:1-23

1 *And all the people of Judah took Uzziah, who was sixteen years old, and made him king in the place of his father Amaziah.*

2 *He built Eloth and restored it to Judah after the king slept with his fathers.*

3 *Uzziah was sixteen years old when he became king, and he reigned fifty-two years in Jerusalem; and his mother's name was Jechiliah of Jerusalem.*

4 He did right in the sight of the LORD according to all that his father Amaziah had done.

5 He continued to seek God in the days of Zechariah, who had understanding through the vision of God; and as long as he sought the LORD, God prospered him.

6 Now he went out and warred against the Philistines, and broke down the wall of Gath and the wall of Jabneh and the wall of Ashdod; and he built cities in the area of Ashdod and among the Philistines.

7 God helped him against the Philistines, and against the Arabians who lived in Gur-baal, and the Meunites.

8 The Ammonites also gave tribute to Uzziah, and his fame extended to the border of Egypt, for he became very strong.

9 Moreover, Uzziah built towers in Jerusalem at the Corner Gate and at the Valley Gate and at the corner buttress and fortified them.

10 He built towers in the wilderness and hewed many cisterns, for he had much livestock, both in the lowland and in the plain. He also had plowmen and vinedressers in the hill country and the fertile fields, for he loved the soil.

11 Moreover, Uzziah had an army ready for battle, which entered combat by divisions according to the number of their muster, prepared by Jeiel the scribe and Maaseiah the official, under the direction of Hananiah, one of the king's officers.

12 The total number of the heads of the households, of valiant warriors, was 2,600.

13 Under their direction was an elite army of 307,500, who could wage war with great power, to help the king against the enemy.

14 Moreover, Uzziah prepared for all the army shields, spears, helmets, body armor, bows and sling stones.

15 In Jerusalem he made engines of war invented by skillful men to be on the towers and on the corners for the purpose of shooting arrows and great stones. Hence his fame spread afar, for he was marvelously helped until he was strong.

16 But when he became strong, his heart was so proud that he acted corruptly, and he was unfaithful to the LORD his God, for he entered the temple of the LORD to burn incense on the altar of incense.

17 Then Azariah the priest entered after him and with him eighty priests of the LORD, valiant men.

18 They opposed Uzziah the king and said to him, "It is not for you, Uzziah, to burn incense to the LORD, but for the priests, the sons of Aaron who are consecrated to burn incense. Get out of the sanctuary, for you have been unfaithful and will have no honor from the LORD God."

19 But Uzziah, with a censer in his hand for burning incense, was enraged; and while he was enraged with the priests, the leprosy broke out on his forehead before the priests in the house of the LORD, beside the altar of incense.

20 Azariah the chief priest and all the priests looked at him, and behold, he was leprous on his forehead; and they hurried him out of there, and he himself also hastened to get out because the LORD had smitten him.

21 King Uzziah was a leper to the day of his death; and he lived in a separate house, being a leper, for he was cut off from the house of the LORD. And Jotham his son was over the king's house judging the people of the land.

22 Now the rest of the acts of Uzziah, first to last, the prophet Isaiah, the son of Amoz, has written.

23 So Uzziah slept with his fathers, and they buried him with his fathers in the field of the grave which belonged to the kings, for they said, "He is a leper." And Jotham his son became king in his place.

DISCUSS with your GROUP or PONDER on your own . . .

Compare your lists from 2 Kings 15 and 2 Chronicles 26. What facts are repeated from 2 Kings 15?

What does the Chronicler add about Uzziah's seeking after God? When did he seek God? Who influenced him in this? What resulted?

What does this demonstrate regarding Uzziah's heart at this point in his life? What types of input was he open to? Explain.

What is your heart like? Are you willing to submit yourself to seeking God and listening to counsel from others who seek Him? Explain.

Verses 6–15 document the height of Uzziah's reign. What characterized it?

Why was Uzziah so successful? Why did his fame grow and spread?

What do you think it was like to live in Uzziah's kingdom? Why?

What happened to Uzziah's heart when he became strong? What did he subsequently do? How are his actions described in verse 16?

Can you relate to Uzziah? Has your heart ever changed when you became more established or more "powerful"? If so, what happened?

Was the power or position in and of itself the problem? Why/why not? Explain from Scripture.

In what context of Israel's national and spiritual life does Uzziah sin?

Who opposes the king and how do they go about it?

Who has the king offended? What clear commands did he disobey?

How does Uzziah respond? What happens?

How has Uzziah's heart changed from what it had been?

How do you respond when people confront you with truth? Are you quick to listen or quick to fight? What does your typical response say about the state of your heart?

Did God judge Uzziah immediately or give him an opportunity to repent? Explain your answer.

ONE STEP FURTHER:

"Be Strong and Courageous!"
If you have some extra time this week, read Joshua 1 and consider God's repeated command to Joshua to "be strong and courageous." Consider this question: *How does this command differ from what Uzziah became?* Then, record your thoughts below.

Week Two: **Wrong Perception, Wrong Reality**

When does Uzziah finally "get" what's going on?

Does a leper have any hope for entering the house of the LORD? For living a normal life? How will this fundamentally change Uzziah's life?

How will the truths you've learned about Uzziah's life change the way you think and act this week?

THE PROPHETS

OBSERVE the TEXT of SCRIPTURE

READ Isaiah 6:1-8 and **MARK** every reference to the *Lord* and every reference to *Isaiah*. Always remember to include synonyms and pronouns.

Isaiah 6:1-8

1 In the year of King Uzziah's death I saw the Lord sitting on a throne, lofty and exalted, with the train of His robe filling the temple.

2 Seraphim stood above Him, each having six wings: with two he covered his face, and with two he covered his feet, and with two he flew.

3 And one called out to another and said,

   "Holy, Holy, Holy, is the LORD of hosts,

   The whole earth is full of His glory."

4 And the foundations of the thresholds trembled at the voice of him who called out, while the temple was filling with smoke.

5 Then I said,

   "Woe is me, for I am ruined!

   Because I am a man of unclean lips,

   And I live among a people of unclean lips;

   For my eyes have seen the King, the LORD of hosts."

Notes

Digging Deeper

Seeking God

Uzziah prospered when he sought God, but the wheels fell off when he started believing his own press. If you have some extra time this week, see what you can discover about the concept of "seeking God" by searching the Scriptures for what they say about the topic. See what different Hebrew and Greek words are used, what contexts you find the concept in, and how you can apply these biblical truths in your own life.

FYI:

Too open-ended?

The goal of open-ended questions—particularly in **Digging Deeper** sections—is to challenge you to think for yourself without depending on prompts. Over time this will help you reason through the text more and more independently. Often we discover more when we're given more room to ask questions and explore. If you only have to fill in a blank, that's about how much you'll learn . . . but if you're given a page, oh my, the possibilities are endless!

6 *Then one of the seraphim flew to me with a burning coal in his hand, which he had taken from the altar with tongs.*

7 *He touched my mouth with it and said, "Behold, this has touched your lips; and your iniquity is taken away and your sin is forgiven."*

8 *Then I heard the voice of the Lord, saying, "Whom shall I send, and who will go for Us?" Then I said, "Here am I. Send me!"*

DISCUSS with your GROUP or PONDER on your own . . .

What historical event opens this chapter?

What encounter does Isaiah describe? Who and what does he see and hear?

What does this text teach about the Lord? Make a simple list based on your marking.

How do those around the throne respond to the Lord?

How does Isaiah respond to this vision of the Lord? How does this clear picture of God affect Isaiah's view of himself?

How do you view yourself primarily—in light of others' opinions or in light of who God is? What impacts does each have?

How does Isaiah view himself in relation to others? How does he pray for himself and them?

How do you view others? Do you see yourself as "above" them or as "one of them"? How does this impact how you relate to them? Explain.

How did you come to your view of God? How do you know it is true?

Compare Uzziah's approach to God with Isaiah's encounter. Note specifically how their attitudes change after God meets them.

Have you ever been paralyzed by guilt from something you did in the past? Was Isaiah paralyzed by the revelation of his sin? Why/why not? What happened to him?

What happens to Isaiah when he views himself correctly? What does God do for him? What does this prepare him to do?

SETTING the SCENE

While captive in Babylon, the prophet Daniel identifies with his unclean people as Isaiah had done years before.

OBSERVE the TEXT of SCRIPTURE

READ Daniel 9:1-9 and **MARK** every place Daniel includes himself with the sinful people of Judah. (You're looking for *we, us, our*, etc.)

Daniel 9:1-9

1   *In the first year of Darius the son of Ahasuerus, of Median descent, who was made king over the kingdom of the Chaldeans—*

2   *in the first year of his reign, I, Daniel, observed in the books the number of the years which was* revealed as *the word of the LORD to Jeremiah the prophet for the completion of the desolations of Jerusalem,* namely, *seventy years.*

3   *So I gave my attention to the Lord God to seek* Him by *prayer and supplications, with fasting, sackcloth and ashes.*

4   *I prayed to the LORD my God and confessed and said, "Alas, O Lord, the great and awesome God, who keeps His covenant and lovingkindness for those who love Him and keep His commandments,*

5   *we have sinned, committed iniquity, acted wickedly and rebelled, even turning aside from Your commandments and ordinances.*

6   *"Moreover, we have not listened to Your servants the prophets, who spoke in Your name to our kings, our princes, our fathers and all the people of the land.*

7   *"Righteousness belongs to You, O Lord, but to us open shame, as it is this day—to the men of Judah, the inhabitants of Jerusalem and all Israel, those who are nearby and those who are far away in all the countries to which You have driven them, because of their unfaithful deeds which they have committed against You.*

8   *"Open shame belongs to us, O Lord, to our kings, our princes and our fathers, because we have sinned against You.*

9   *"To the Lord our God* belong *compassion and forgiveness, for we have rebelled against Him;*

10   *nor have we obeyed the voice of the LORD our God, to walk in His teachings which He set before us through His servants the prophets.*

DISCUSS with your GROUP or PONDER on your own . . .

What causes Daniel to seek God according to this text? How does he go about it?

What sins does he confess? Why?

What can we learn from this text about Daniel's views of God, of others, and of himself that we can apply in our lives?

FYI:

Contemporaries

Like Ezekiel, Daniel wrote from Babylon during Judah's captivity there. Taken as a youth from his homeland, he was trained to serve in King Nebuchadnezzar's court. He was taken captive in 605 BC, the third year of Jehoiakim's reign in Judah (Daniel 1:1-6). Ezekiel wrote from Babylon starting in the fifth year of Jehoiachin's exile, which started in 597 BC after he had reigned only three *months.*

@THE END OF THE DAY . . .

It's not a coincidence that Isaiah's vision of the LORD came the same year King Uzziah died. Uzziah was greatly helped by God but when he became strong and proud God humbled him. Uzziah had a wrong picture of himself and a wrong view of God. Isaiah, by contrast, viewed God and himself rightly as did Daniel, and God made each fit and clean for service. As we close our study this week, spend some time reflecting and praying about what you've learned. Then summarize the most important truth you need to remember in one sentence and jot it down below.

Week Three
Living Unentitled in a Me-First Culture

God is opposed to the proud, but gives grace to the humble.
–James 4:6b

Uzziah started well. He didn't start off with pride problems. He grew into them as his power grew. Certain cultures, however, nurture and feed pride from the womb. As we return to our friend John the Baptist, we'll see how he lived an unentitled life devoted to God and His purposes and how God graciously cultivates humility in lives.

REMEMBERING

What have you learned so far?

OBSERVE the TEXT of SCRIPTURE

READ Luke 1–7 (yes, the chapters) and Mark 6:14-32. Although the Luke reading will give much information about Jesus and John, don't skip or skim as it will help greatly in understanding the context. As you read this section look for the big picture and don't get bogged down in details yet. We'll get to them all in due time.

As you read, simply observe the text and jot down questions you have. Asking good questions is core to good Bible study. Exegesis, the fifty-cent word for Bible study, simply means to "draw out." Asking relevant questions is the first step in drawing the meaning out of the text. Learning to ask your own questions as opposed to answering ones others put to you is a critical step in learning to feed yourself God's Word and hone the skills that feed others and teach them to do the same.

Questions on Luke 1-7:

Questions on Mark 6:14-32:

What is the general context—when do the events happen and where?

Besides John the Baptist, what major players in these chapters help us understand John better? You may want to circle or highlight these individuals as you read.

If you have time, record minor players and the names just mentioned in passing. If you don't have the time, move on. Again, you may want to underline or highlight these people in a different color.

Looking back over your lists of people, which ones do you think deserve more investigation and why?

INDUCTIVE FOCUS:

Using Your Own Symbols

Marking the text will help key words stand out but the method of **marking** you use (if you choose to **mark** at all) is entirely up to you. You may prefer colors to symbols or a larger font which you can scale up on a computer. Whatever you choose, always remember that **marking** is a means to the end of understanding the text and never an end in itself. Always remember to use the tool and *not* let the tool rule you!

Moving from "What it Says" to "What it Means" to "How it Applies"

We've spent a lot of time this week observing Scripture and asking questions to help us discover for ourselves what the text says and means. Applying a text correctly depends on the correct interpretation. Yes, we can apply a text a variety of ways to different situations in life, but every application must be grounded in what the text says in its original context. This bothers people who want the text to say what they think it says. But if a text says and means only what we arbitrarily feel or think it says or means, we can easily lose its true meaning.

Have you ever been in a heated conflict when your opponent defended their actions or words with "But I thought you said . . . " or "I thought you meant . . . "? If so, you've experienced both bad listening and interpreting.

We can have the same problems listening to and interpreting God's Word that we have in everyday conversation so we have to learn how to observe and interpret carefully.

ZACHARIAS AND ELIZABETH

Now that we've overviewed the entire life of John the Baptist recorded by Luke, let's move in for a closer look at the beginning of his story, the story that God ordained and orchestrated even prior to his birth. Of all the Gospel accounts, Luke alone gives us his backstory. The man Jesus referred to as greater than any born of women was born into a significant extended family. John, as we will see, grew up with godly influences. The plan for his life was marked out before he was conceived!

OBSERVE the TEXT of SCRIPTURE

READ Luke 1 in your Bible or use the text included at the end of the lesson. As you read, you may want to use different colored pencils to mark references to the main characters. This can be especially helpful for visual learners. Since we'll be reading through Luke 1 several times this week, on the first read **MARK** in a distinctive fashion all references to *Zacharias* and *Elizabeth*.

DISCUSS with your GROUP or PONDER on your own . . .

Summarize the main points of Luke 1. Don't go crazy, just recap the highlights as if you were telling the story to a friend.

Who are the main players in Luke 1 and how does each one relate to John? In what way or ways is each significant?

Take some time to compile a simple list of everything you learned about John's parents, Zacharias and Elizabeth. Be sure to record where you found the material as shown below. It makes for easier discussion.

Zacharias	Elizabeth
priest, v. 5	wife of Zacharias, v. 5

FYI:

Think on this . . .

Some scholars think that Luke interviewed Mary, one of the eyewitnesses to the events he recorded in his Gospel account. Certainly he wrote under the inspiration of the Holy Spirit, but that does not rule out investigating eyewitness accounts to events he refers to in the opening verses Luke 1.

Notes

Based on the facts you compiled and the lists you made, how would you characterize Zacharias and Elizabeth?

What life situations that you see in the text could have set them up for a sense of "better-than-thou-ness" or "entitlement"?

In what ways can "position" cause us to feel entitled?

Is there anything in your life that woos (or has wooed) you into "better-than-thou" or entitlement thinking? Do you or any family members hold special positions that are looked upon especially well either in society-at-large or in your particular social groups? Is there anything about your family's heritage that is more remarkable than most? Explain.

Does the presence or absence of this affect the way you think and act today? If so, how? Before you say, "It doesn't," ask God to reveal to you any subtle ways entitlement thinking may be affecting you.

Do you find yourself seeking prominent positions more or less than you did five years ago? Ten years ago? If this has changed over the years, how has it changed and why do you think it has?

ONE STEP FURTHER:

Investigating the priesthood . . .

We're told that the angel appeared to Zacharias by the altar of incense. Do you know what else was in the temple besides this altar? How much do you know about the priesthood of the Old Testament? Was it significant that the coming Messiah be heralded by a Levitic priest? If you have time see what you can discover about the Levitic priesthood by investigating cross-references and other resource tools such as a Bible dictionary. Then record your findings below.

Let's face it, to be the priest offering incense or a wife of "the daughters of Aaron" (as the text notes) was certainly notable in first-century Jewish culture. What, however, does the text specifically say about their character in verse 6?

TRUE STORES:

One barren woman and two entitled sons . . .

If you are able this week, take some time to consider 1 Samuel 1-4. In it you'll find the account of another once-barren woman whom God blessed with a son, as well as the tragic account of the priest Eli and his "entitled" sons. Does the text tell us why they acted the way they did? How does the behavior of Eli and his sons differ from that of Zacharias? If you have time to read widely, continue reading through 1 Samuel 8:1-9 and consider the outcome of Samuel's sons as well. Record your observations below.

What specific situations or events in the lives of Zacharias and Elizabeth may have cultivated an attitude of humility in them? Explain.

How did Zacharias and Elizabeth respond to trying situations and events in their lives? Note specific verses as you answer.

Have there been events in your life in which God cultivated a spirit of humility in you? If you can, recount a specific instance. How did you respond?

Take some time to sit quietly or go for a walk with God and ponder the story of Zacharias and Elizabeth. Ask God to cement one specific truth to your heart and write that truth below.

MARY

OBSERVE the TEXT of SCRIPTURE

READ Luke 1 again, this time **MARKING** every reference to *Mary*.

DISCUSS with your GROUP or PONDER on your own . . .

Take a few minutes to summarize everything you learned about Mary in Luke 1. You can make a simple list like we did with Zacharias and Elizabeth or write out a short summary paragraph. As you compile your information actively think through it—don't just record facts. Particularly consider and note information that you may not have noticed before. Stick to the text, but reason as you go.

Take some time to compare Elizabeth and Mary's situations. How were they similar? In what ways did they differ?

Describe Elizabeth's interaction with Mary. What, if anything, stands out in her behavior?

While we're at it, compare Mary and Zacharias's encounters with Gabriel. What is similar? What differs?

ONE STEP FURTHER:

Thinking through the Scriptures . . .

How does Zacharias stack up in comparison to other priests and Levites throughout Israel's history? Think through the full counsel of God's Word and use whatever resources you have available to you to answer. Record your findings below.

How does Mary respond to the angel? How does she describe herself?

While both Zacharias and Mary aligned themselves with God's plan, the old priest had some initial doubts. Consider for a moment *your* willingness to live as God's bond slave. For Mary obedience meant a very public, life-long humiliation. People would undoubtedly point, stare and talk about her disparagingly if she chose to submit to God's perfect plan. Yet in spite of the threat of permanent public disgrace she submitted . . . immediately!

Here's the question: *When it's hard and potentially humiliating, how am I at obeying immediately and fully?*

OBSERVE the TEXT of SCRIPTURE

Let's look a little more closely at Mary's words recorded in Luke 1.

READ Luke 1:46-55. As you do, **MARK** every word associated with humility (*humble, bondslave,* etc.). Also **MARK** every reference to *God.*

DISCUSS with your GROUP or PONDER on your own . . .

Looking back at the words associated with humility, summarize what Mary says about it. What does the text say about pride?

Describe Mary's view of herself.

Describe Mary's view of God. What is her view of herself in relation to God? Watch what the text says; don't go from "what you've always been told."

What does this text say about moving up and down in God's economy?

What is your view of yourself in relation to God? Explain.

Take some time to prayerfully consider the following question: In order to align yourself more with what Mary says about God in this text, what changes do you need to make?

Digging Deeper

Pride, Humility and other Related Topics

If you have some extra time this week, roll up your sleeves and do a little research on your own. See what else you can discover about pride and humility by searching your concordance on related terms. This will be a good exercise in thinking about how to find material you're looking for. Here are a few terms to get you started:

Pride (exalted, lifted up . . .)

Humility (humble, low, cast down . . .)

What I discovered . . .

GOD'S VIEW

OBSERVE the TEXT of SCRIPTURE

In studying Luke 1 we've been encountering humble people and their views of God. Before we finish for the week, let's take some time to explore God's views of people—proud and humble.

READ Proverbs 3:34, James 4:6, and 1 Peter 5:5 and **MARK** in a distinctive fashion every reference to *proud* and *humble*. Don't forget to include synonyms.

Proverbs 3:34 (NASB)

34 Though He scoffs at the scoffers,

Yet He gives grace to the afflicted.

Proverbs 3:34 (ESV)

34 Toward the scorners he is scornful,

but to the humble he gives favor.

James 4:6-10

6 But He gives a greater grace. Therefore it says, "GOD IS OPPOSED TO THE PROUD, BUT GIVES GRACE TO THE HUMBLE."

7 Submit therefore to God. Resist the devil and he will flee from you.

8 Draw near to God and He will draw near to you. Cleanse your hands, you sinners; and purify your hearts, you double-minded.

9 Be miserable and mourn and weep; let your laughter be turned into mourning and your joy to gloom.

10 Humble yourselves in the presence of the Lord, and He will exalt you.

1 Peter 5:5-7

5 You younger men, likewise, be subject to your elders; and all of you, clothe yourselves with humility toward one another, for GOD IS OPPOSED TO THE PROUD, BUT GIVES GRACE TO THE HUMBLE.

6 Therefore humble yourselves under the mighty hand of God, that He may exalt you at the proper time,

7 casting all your anxiety on Him, because He cares for you.

DISCUSS with your GROUP or PONDER on your own . . .

How does God act toward the proud and the scoffers of the world?

Notes

FYI:

"Opposed"

"Opposed" in James and 1 Peter (*antitasso*) literally means "to arrange [or 'order'] against."

Conversely, what does He do for the humble?

What are some practical ways we can seek to live humble lives that please God? What benefits come with a life of humility according to the texts?

@ the End of the Day . . .

Zacharias, Elizabeth, and Mary all walked humbly with their God. Elizabeth endured years of barrenness and Zacharias lived nine months mute, but both knew their God. Certainly these life experiences fostered humility in the old couple. Whereas a miraculous late-in-life birth cultivated humility in Elizabeth, Mary chose to humble herself before God, submitting immediately to the hard obedience of carrying our Lord and Savior Jesus, the Son of God in a virgin womb.

OBSERVATION WORKSHEET

Luke 1

1 *Inasmuch as many have undertaken to compile an account of the things accomplished among us,*

2 *just as they were handed down to us by those who from the beginning were eyewitnesses and servants of the word,*

3 *it seemed fitting for me as well, having investigated everything carefully from the beginning, to write it out for you in consecutive order, most excellent Theophilus;*

4 *so that you may know the exact truth about the things you have been taught.*

5 *In the days of Herod, king of Judea, there was a priest named Zacharias, of the division of Abijah; and he had a wife from the daughters of Aaron, and her name was Elizabeth.*

6 *They were both righteous in the sight of God, walking blamelessly in all the commandments and requirements of the Lord.*

7 *But they had no child, because Elizabeth was barren, and they were both advanced in years.*

8 *Now it happened that while he was performing his priestly service before God in the appointed order of his division,*

9 *according to the custom of the priestly office, he was chosen by lot to enter the temple of the Lord and burn incense.*

10 *And the whole multitude of the people were in prayer outside at the hour of the incense offering.*

11 *And an angel of the Lord appeared to him, standing to the right of the altar of incense.*

12 *Zacharias was troubled when he saw the angel, and fear gripped him.*

13 *But the angel said to him, "Do not be afraid, Zacharias, for your petition has been heard, and your wife Elizabeth will bear you a son, and you will give him the name John.*

14 *"You will have joy and gladness, and many will rejoice at his birth.*

15 *"For he will be great in the sight of the Lord; and he will drink no wine or liquor, and he will be filled with the Holy Spirit while yet in his mother's womb.*

16 *"And he will turn many of the sons of Israel back to the Lord their God.*

17 *"It is he who will go as a forerunner before Him in the spirit and power of Elijah, TO TURN THE HEARTS OF THE FATHERS BACK TO THE CHILDREN, and the disobedient to the attitude of the righteous, so as to make ready a people prepared for the Lord."*

18 *Zacharias said to the angel, "How will I know this for certain? For I am an old man and my wife is advanced in years."*

19 The angel answered and said to him, "I am Gabriel, who stands in the presence of God, and I have been sent to speak to you and to bring you this good news.

20 "And behold, you shall be silent and unable to speak until the day when these things take place, because you did not believe my words, which will be fulfilled in their proper time."

21 The people were waiting for Zacharias, and were wondering at his delay in the temple.

22 But when he came out, he was unable to speak to them; and they realized that he had seen a vision in the temple; and he kept making signs to them, and remained mute.

23 When the days of his priestly service were ended, he went back home.

24 After these days Elizabeth his wife became pregnant, and she kept herself in seclusion for five months, saying,

25 "This is the way the Lord has dealt with me in the days when He looked with favor upon me, to take away my disgrace among men."

26 Now in the sixth month the angel Gabriel was sent from God to a city in Galilee called Nazareth,

27 to a virgin engaged to a man whose name was Joseph, of the descendants of David; and the virgin's name was Mary.

28 And coming in, he said to her, "Greetings, favored one! The Lord is with you."

29 But she was very perplexed at this statement, and kept pondering what kind of salutation this was.

30 The angel said to her, "Do not be afraid, Mary; for you have found favor with God.

31 "And behold, you will conceive in your womb and bear a son, and you shall name Him Jesus.

32 "He will be great and will be called the Son of the Most High; and the Lord God will give Him the throne of His father David;

33 and He will reign over the house of Jacob forever, and His kingdom will have no end."

34 Mary said to the angel, "How can this be, since I am a virgin?"

35 The angel answered and said to her, "The Holy Spirit will come upon you, and the power of the Most High will overshadow you; and for that reason the holy Child shall be called the Son of God.

36 "And behold, even your relative Elizabeth has also conceived a son in her old age; and she who was called barren is now in her sixth month.

37 "For nothing will be impossible with God."

38 And Mary said, "Behold, the bondslave of the Lord; may it be done to me according to your word." And the angel departed from her.

39 Now at this time Mary arose and went in a hurry to the hill country, to a city of Judah,

40 and entered the house of Zacharias and greeted Elizabeth.

41 When Elizabeth heard Mary's greeting, the baby leaped in her womb; and Elizabeth was filled with the Holy Spirit.

42 And she cried out with a loud voice and said, "Blessed are you among women, and blessed is the fruit of your womb!

43 "And how has it happened to me, that the mother of my Lord would come to me?

44 "For behold, when the sound of your greeting reached my ears, the baby leaped in my womb for joy.

45 "And blessed is she who believed that there would be a fulfillment of what had been spoken to her by the Lord."

46 And Mary said:

"My soul exalts the Lord,

47 And my spirit has rejoiced in God my Savior.

48 "For He has had regard for the humble state of His bondslave;

For behold, from this time on all generations will count me blessed.

49 "For the Mighty One has done great things for me;

And holy is His name.

50 "AND HIS MERCY IS UPON GENERATION AFTER GENERATION

TOWARD THOSE WHO FEAR HIM.

51 "He has done mighty deeds with His arm;

He has scattered those who were proud in the thoughts of their heart.

52 "He has brought down rulers from their thrones,

And has exalted those who were humble.

53 "HE HAS FILLED THE HUNGRY WITH GOOD THINGS;

And sent away the rich empty-handed.

54 "He has given help to Israel His servant,

In remembrance of His mercy,

55 As He spoke to our fathers,

To Abraham and his descendants forever."

56 And Mary stayed with her about three months, and then returned to her home.

57 Now the time had come for Elizabeth to give birth, and she gave birth to a son.

58 Her neighbors and her relatives heard that the Lord had displayed His great mercy toward her; and they were rejoicing with her.

59 And it happened that on the eighth day they came to circumcise the child, and they were going to call him Zacharias, after his father.

60 But his mother answered and said, "No indeed; but he shall be called John."

61 And they said to her, "There is no one among your relatives who is called by that name."

62   *And they made signs to his father, as to what he wanted him called.*

63   *And he asked for a tablet and wrote as follows, "His name is John." And they were all astonished.*

64   *And at once his mouth was opened and his tongue loosed, and he began to speak in praise of God.*

65   *Fear came on all those living around them; and all these matters were being talked about in all the hill country of Judea.*

66   *All who heard them kept them in mind, saying, "What then will this child turn out to be?" For the hand of the Lord was certainly with him.*

67   *And his father Zacharias was filled with the Holy Spirit, and prophesied, saying:*

68   *"Blessed be the Lord God of Israel,*

For He has visited us and accomplished redemption for His people,

69   *And has raised up a horn of salvation for us*

In the house of David His servant—

70   *As He spoke by the mouth of His holy prophets from of old—*

71   *Salvation FROM OUR ENEMIES,*

And FROM THE HAND OF ALL WHO HATE US;

72   *To show mercy toward our fathers,*

And to remember His holy covenant,

73   *The oath which He swore to Abraham our father,*

74   *To grant us that we, being rescued from the hand of our enemies,*

Might serve Him without fear,

75   *In holiness and righteousness before Him all our days.*

76   *"And you, child, will be called the prophet of the Most High;*

For you will go on BEFORE THE LORD TO PREPARE HIS WAYS;

77   *To give to His people the knowledge of salvation*

By the forgiveness of their sins,

78   *Because of the tender mercy of our God,*

With which the Sunrise from on high will visit us,

79   *TO SHINE UPON THOSE WHO SIT IN DARKNESS AND THE SHADOW OF DEATH,*

To guide our feet into the way of peace."

80   *And the child continued to grow and to become strong in spirit, and he lived in the deserts until the day of his public appearance to Israel.*

FYI:

Old Testament Quotations

When a New Testament author quotes from the Old Testament, it's always helpful to go back and read the quotation in its original context. In the NASB, you'll notice that Old Testament quotations are set in CAPITAL LETTERS.

Week Four

Upside Down: Living Like John and Jesus

"For even the Son of Man did not come to be served, but to serve, and to give His life a ransom for many."
—Jesus, Mark 10:45

John decreased as Jesus increased. But that's not the whole story. Jesus' "increase" according to the predetermined plan of God led Him first to the cross but then, in victory over death, to heaven and the right hand of God. In the greatest story ever told, the God of the universe took on flesh to serve, to sacrifice, and to save His sinful, rebellious creation. Both Jesus and John flipped their culture's worldview on its head and set the example for you and me to follow!

REMEMBERING

Since our minds tend to leak a bit, take some time to review what you've learned so far. Start by listing the major points we've covered and then make it personal by recording where God has been working in your life.

ONE STEP FURTHER:

Examine the Quoted Texts
If you have some extra time this week, see if you can identify Old Testament passages quoted in Luke 1. When you find them, explore them in their original contexts and record your observations below.

OBSERVE the TEXT of SCRIPTURE

READ through the text of Luke 1 again. This time **MARK** every reference you see to *John the Baptist* and to *Jesus.* Be sure to include synonyms and pronouns.

DISCUSS with your GROUP or PONDER on your own . . .

How would you characterize what is going on in Luke 1 in the context of first-century Judaism? Is it "same old, same old" or something else? Why is this significant?

Now, having marked references to John and Jesus compile your information into a simple list so you can compare them. Remember to record the verses where you found the information as you go to make discussion time easier.

John	Jesus

In what ways were the birth announcements similar? How did they differ?

By human standards, which child should have been the more honored of the two and why?

By human standards, what should John the Baptist have been named and why?

By human standards, what should John have grown up to be?

By human standards, what could have wooed John towards feelings of entitlement?

When you succumb to feelings of entitlement or self-centeredness how does it show in *your* behaviors? What does it take for you to become aware that it's going on?

Spend some time asking God to reveal thoughts and behaviors that are rooted in entitlement thinking. Record these below.

FYI:

Are you remembering to pray?

In John 16:13 Jesus tells His disciples that when the Spirit of truth comes, He will guide them into all the truth. It's important for us to remember to ask the Father to teach and guide us by His Holy Spirit as we study the Word. It's easy to become self-centered even in a Bible study, particularly if we're long-time students and think we have it all under control.

Remember that Jesus taught His disciples to fix their eyes on God and His holiness (Matthew 6:9-10) before they actually ask Him for things. That is where a right view of prayer begins.

OBSERVE the TEXT of SCRIPTURE

READ Luke 1 again. This time **MARK** every reference to *God*. Distinguish the ways you mark references to *the Father, the Son,* and *the Holy Spirit.*

DISCUSS with your GROUP or PONDER on your own . . .

Make a simple list of God's actions, purposes, and plan.

From Luke 1, describe:
God the Father

God the Son

God the Holy Spirit

Whose purposes are being accomplished in Luke 1? What are the people doing when God "enters the scene"? What does He call them to do?

Are you carrying worries today? If so, are there things you are trying to "make happen"? Are there things you are trying to "do for God"? If so, name them and write them down.

Based on what we have seen in Luke 1, how much control do you have? How much control does God have? Do you ever blur these lines? If so, how?

Digging Deeper

Contemporary Application: Life of the Unborn

Luke tells his readers that the angel Gabriel appeared to both Elizabeth and Mary announcing the birth of two babies before either of them had been conceived. What does this suggest about the beginning of life?

If you have time this week, search the Scriptures for what God says about when life begins. If you're not sure where to go, consider Jeremiah and the Psalms among others.

Taking this from another angle, what does God say about the weak and helpless? What does He say about those who harm them?

How does this issue relate to living in a "selfie" world? How has it contributed to the growth of the "selfie" mentality? What is the answer? How do we communicate it?

Week Four: **Upside Down: Living Like John and Jesus**

OBSERVE the TEXT of SCRIPTURE

Luke 1 gives John's backstory and records Gabriel's announcement to Mary that she will bear a son. Luke 2 recounts Jesus' birth, His presentation at the temple as a baby, and His Passover visit to Jerusalem at age 12. At the beginning of Luke 3, time has passed and the Word of God comes to a now-grown John . . . which is where we'll pick up the account.

READ Luke 3:1-22 and **MARK** every reference to *John* including pronouns.
UNDERLINE every instruction he gives.

Luke 3:1-22

1 Now in the fifteenth year of the reign of Tiberius Caesar, when Pontius Pilate was governor of Judea, and Herod was tetrarch of Galilee, and his brother Philip was tetrarch of the region of Ituraea and Trachonitis, and Lysanias was tetrarch of Abilene,

2 in the high priesthood of Annas and Caiaphas, the word of God came to John, the son of Zacharias, in the wilderness.

3 And he came into all the district around the Jordan, preaching a baptism of repentance for the forgiveness of sins;

4 as it is written in the book of the words of Isaiah the prophet,

   "THE VOICE OF ONE CRYING IN THE WILDERNESS,

   'MAKE READY THE WAY OF THE LORD,

   MAKE HIS PATHS STRAIGHT.

5 *'EVERY RAVINE WILL BE FILLED,*

   AND EVERY MOUNTAIN AND HILL WILL BE BROUGHT LOW;

   THE CROOKED WILL BECOME STRAIGHT,

   AND THE ROUGH ROADS SMOOTH;

6 *AND ALL FLESH WILL SEE THE SALVATION OF GOD.' "*

7 So he began *saying* to the crowds who were going out to be baptized by him, "You brood of vipers, who warned you to flee from the wrath to come?

8 "Therefore bear fruits in keeping with repentance, and do not begin to say to yourselves, 'We have Abraham for our father,' for I say to you that from these stones God is able to raise up children to Abraham.

9 "Indeed the axe is already laid at the root of the trees; so every tree that does not bear good fruit is cut down and thrown into the fire."

10 And the crowds were questioning him, saying, "Then what shall we do?"

11 And he would answer and say to them, "The man who has two tunics is to share with him who has none; and he who has food is to do likewise."

12 And some *tax collectors* also came to be baptized, and they said to him, "Teacher, what shall we do?"

13 And he said to them, "Collect no more than what you have been ordered to."

14 Some *soldiers* were questioning him, saying, "And what about *us,* what shall we do?" And he said to them, "Do not take money from anyone by force, or accuse anyone falsely, and be content with your wages."

15 *Now while the people were in a state of expectation and all were wondering in their hearts about John, as to whether he was the Christ,*

16 *John answered and said to them all, "As for me, I baptize you with water; but One is coming who is mightier than I, and I am not fit to untie the thong of His sandals; He will baptize you with the Holy Spirit and fire.*

17 *"His winnowing fork is in His hand to thoroughly clear His threshing floor, and to gather the wheat into His barn; but He will burn up the chaff with unquenchable fire."*

18 *So with many other exhortations he preached the gospel to the people.*

19 *But when Herod the tetrarch was reprimanded by him because of Herodias, his brother's wife, and because of all the wicked things which Herod had done,*

20 *Herod also added this to them all: he locked John up in prison.*

21 *Now when all the people were baptized, Jesus was also baptized, and while He was praying, heaven was opened,*

22 *and the Holy Spirit descended upon Him in bodily form like a dove, and a voice came out of heaven, "You are My beloved Son, in You I am well-pleased."*

DISCUSS with your GROUP or PONDER on your own . . .

Record your general observations on Luke 3:1-22.

Note both the civil and religious rulers mentioned in Luke 3:1-2. Who are they? Where do they rule? How many are mentioned in total?

Although there are many rulers in place, who does the Word of God come to and where?

What is John's message to the people? Where in the Old Testament does Luke quote from? What is his point?

Digging Deeper

The Rest of the Story on John the Baptist

If you have extra time this week, do some more digging into John the Baptist's life by looking at the records in Matthew 3 and Mark 1:1-15. Cross-referencing and comparing parallel accounts can help us fill in details. Remember, Scripture interprets Scripture. The best commentary on the Bible is the Word of God itself. Here are a few questions to help get you started as you consider the Matthew and Mark accounts.

What are your general observations on Matthew 3? What additional information did you learn from Matthew that you did not find out from Luke?

What are your general observations on Mark 1:1-15? Did you learn anything from this account that was unique in comparison with the accounts of Luke and Matthew?

According to these passages, what did John eat? What did he wear? What do you think is significant about these things?

By way of application, if you did not have to worry about what you were going to eat or wear, how many purposeful hours would that add to your day? Your week?

Without going crazy here, can you think of any ways to simplify what you eat and wear to free up time to "increase" God's business and "decrease" your own?

What are other ways can you simplify your life?

OBSERVE the TEXT of SCRIPTURE

As you read John's Gospel remember that it takes a different approach from the rest. The other three (Matthew, Mark, and Luke) are referred to as the Synoptic (literally "same view") Gospels whereas John's Gospel is written around a series of seven miracles.

READ John 1:1-34 and **MARK** distinctively references to *John* and to *Jesus* including their respective pronouns.

John 1:1-34

1   *In the beginning was the Word, and the Word was with God, and the Word was God.*

2   *He was in the beginning with God.*

3   *All things came into being through Him, and apart from Him nothing came into being that has come into being.*

4   *In Him was life, and the life was the Light of men.*

5   *The Light shines in the darkness, and the darkness did not comprehend it.*

6   *There came a man sent from God, whose name was John.*

7   *He came as a witness, to testify about the Light, so that all might believe through him.*

8   *He was not the Light, but he came to testify about the Light.*

9   *There was the true Light which, coming into the world, enlightens every man.*

10 *He was in the world, and the world was made through Him, and the world did not know Him.*

11 *He came to His own, and those who were His own did not receive Him.*

12 *But as many as received Him, to them He gave the right to become children of God, even to those who believe in His name,*

13 *who were born, not of blood nor of the will of the flesh nor of the will of man, but of God.*

14 *And the Word became flesh, and dwelt among us, and we saw His glory, glory as of the only begotten from the Father, full of grace and truth.*

15 *John *testified about Him and cried out, saying, "This was He of whom I said, 'He who comes after me has a higher rank than I, for He existed before me.' "*

16 *For of His fullness we have all received, and grace upon grace.*

17 *For the Law was given through Moses; grace and truth were realized through Jesus Christ.*

18 *No one has seen God at any time; the only begotten God who is in the bosom of the Father, He has explained Him.*

19 *This is the testimony of John, when the Jews sent to him priests and Levites from Jerusalem to ask him, "Who are you?"*

20 *And he confessed and did not deny, but confessed, "I am not the Christ."*

21 *They asked him, "What then? Are you Elijah?" And he *said, "I am not." "Are you the Prophet?" And he answered, "No."*

INDUCTIVE FOCUS:

Marking Time Phrases
Observing and marking time phrases also helps us understand the text we're reading. Watch for words like *beginning, before, after, now, then, day,* and other time-related words and mark them in a consistent fashion as you read.

22 Then they said to him, "Who are you, so that we may give an answer to those who sent us? What do you say about yourself?"

23 He said, "I am A VOICE OF ONE CRYING IN THE WILDERNESS, 'MAKE STRAIGHT THE WAY OF THE LORD,' as Isaiah the prophet said."

24 Now they had been sent from the Pharisees.

25 They asked him, and said to him, "Why then are you baptizing, if you are not the Christ, nor Elijah, nor the Prophet?"

26 John answered them saying, "I baptize in water, but among you stands One whom you do not know.

27 "It is He who comes after me, the thong of whose sandal I am not worthy to untie."

28 These things took place in Bethany beyond the Jordan, where John was baptizing.

29 The next day he *saw Jesus coming to him and *said, "Behold, the Lamb of God who takes away the sin of the world!

30 "This is He on behalf of whom I said, 'After me comes a Man who has a higher rank than I, for He existed before me.'

31 "I did not recognize Him, but so that He might be manifested to Israel, I came baptizing in water."

32 John testified saying, "I have seen the Spirit descending as a dove out of heaven, and He remained upon Him.

33 "I did not recognize Him, but He who sent me to baptize in water said to me, 'He upon whom you see the Spirit descending and remaining upon Him, this is the One who baptizes in the Holy Spirit.'

34 "I myself have seen, and have testified that this is the Son of God."

DISCUSS with your GROUP or PONDER on your own . . .

What are your general observations on John 1:1-34? What additional information did you learn from this text that you did not find in Luke (or Matthew and Mark, too, if you did the **Digging Deeper**)?

What information was common to John and Luke's Gospels?

Compile a simple list of what John (the Apostle) says about John the Baptist and Jesus. Note the ways in which they are similar and different.

John	Jesus

What was John's purpose? How did he exemplify humility as he carried out his purpose?

What does the text say about the superiority of the Word?

How did the Word exemplify humility? According to the text, who is the Word?

The authors of each of the synoptic Gospels quote Isaiah 40 in reference to John the Baptist. How *specifically* does Isaiah 40 appear in John 1? Why might this be significant?

INDUCTIVE FOCUS:

Doing Your Own Word Study

Doing your own word study involves more than just looking up a word in a Bible dictionary or word study tool. Although these tools are important, the groundwork for a word study involves using a concordance to locate every occurrence of the word and its related word-group members in texts of Scripture and checking them in their contexts. Running to a word study book first is like running to a commentary before reading the text of Scripture.

THE DEITY OF JESUS CHRIST . . .

Evangelical Christianity and truly every orthodox form of Christianity understands John 1 to clearly show the pre-incarnate existence of Jesus, the Word. God incarnate . . . God tabernacling among His people. It is a profound passage that stands alone. However, when considered in the light of Isaiah 40, the passage to which each of the Gospel accounts refers, the argument for the deity of Jesus Christ becomes *even more* compelling! Although the word rendered LORD in John 1:23 is the Greek *kurios*, which can have a rather wide range of meaning, the word translated LORD in Isaiah 40:3 is *YHWH* (meaning *I AM*), the unique name of the God of Israel.

God first discloses His name to Moses in Exodus 3 . . . .

Exodus 3:13-15

Then Moses said to God, "Behold, I am going to the sons of Israel, and I will say to them, 'The God of your fathers has sent me to you.' Now they may say to me, 'What is His name?' What shall I say to them?" God said to Moses, "I AM WHO I AM"; and He said, "Thus you shall say to the sons of Israel, 'I AM has sent me to you.'" God, furthermore, said to Moses, "Thus you shall say to the sons of Israel, 'The LORD, the God of your fathers, the God of Abraham, the God of Isaac, and the God of Jacob, has sent me to you.' This is My name forever, and this is My memorial-name to all generations."

In Isaiah 40:3, we see that the way in the wilderness is being cleared for the LORD, YHWH Himself, the God of Abraham, Isaac, and Israel, the God of Moses, the God of David. Each of the evangelists ties John the Baptist to this passage. Is this a passage with double fulfillment? Quite possibly. Scholars argue on a number of points regarding it, but none argues that at least part of its fulfillment is John the Baptist and his mission of preparing the way of the LORD . . . of Jesus . . . of the Word made flesh.

And when God put on human flesh, He gave us the supreme example of humility that stretches all the way to the cross on our behalf. Let's spend the rest of our time this week looking at some examples of humility in the life of Jesus.

OBSERVE the TEXT of SCRIPTURE

Jesus denounced the cities where He did miracles and the people didn't repent before He made the statements we're looking at below.

READ Matthew 11:25-30 and **MARK** every reference to *Jesus* including pronouns.

Matthew 11:25-30

25 *At that time Jesus said, "I praise You, Father, Lord of heaven and earth, that You have hidden these things from the wise and intelligent and have revealed them to infants.*

26 *"Yes, Father, for this way was well-pleasing in Your sight.*

27 *"All things have been handed over to Me by My Father; and no one knows the Son except the Father; nor does anyone know the Father except the Son, and anyone to whom the Son wills to reveal Him.*

28 *"Come to Me, all who are weary and heavy-laden, and I will give you rest.*

ONE STEP FURTHER:

Get the Whole Story

If you have time this week, get the whole context by reading Matthew 11 then record your observations below.

29 *"Take My yoke upon you and learn from Me, for I am gentle and humble in heart, and YOU WILL FIND REST FOR YOUR SOULS.*

30 *"For My yoke is easy and My burden is light."*

DISCUSS with your GROUP or PONDER on your own . . .

According to Jesus, what is the only way to know the Father? How does this truth appeal to a pluralistic society?

Who is the only one who knows the Father?

What invitation does Jesus give and to who? Does the invitation target everyone or certain kinds of people? How does it relate to the narrow way of knowing the Father?

How does Jesus describe Himself? What does He offer?

Does "gentle and humble in heart" describe your life? If so, how? If not, what is standing in the way?

ONE STEP FURTHER:

Word Study: Gentle

If you have time this week, find the Greek word that is translated "gentle." Where else does it appear in the Gospels? In the New Testament? How else is it translated? How was Jesus "gentle"? Is biblical gentleness on display in *your* life? If so, how?

ONE STEP FURTHER:

Word Study: Humble in Heart

If you have time this week, investigate the Greek phrase translated "humble in heart." See what you can discover and record your findings and applications below.

OBSERVE the TEXT of SCRIPTURE

In the following account, Jesus explains to his disciples James and John what greatness in His kingdom is.

READ Mark 10:35-45 and **MARK** every reference to *James and John*. Then **MARK** every reference to being *great* or *first*.

Mark 10:35-45

35 *James and John, the two sons of Zebedee, came up to Jesus, saying, "Teacher, we want You to do for us whatever we ask of You."*

36 *And He said to them, "What do you want Me to do for you?"*

37 *They said to Him, "Grant that we may sit, one on Your right and one on Your left, in Your glory."*

38 *But Jesus said to them, "You do not know what you are asking. Are you able to drink the cup that I drink, or to be baptized with the baptism with which I am baptized?"*

39 *They said to Him, "We are able." And Jesus said to them, "The cup that I drink you shall drink; and you shall be baptized with the baptism with which I am baptized.*

40 *"But to sit on My right or on My left, this is not Mine to give; but it is for those for whom it has been prepared."*

41 *Hearing this, the ten began to feel indignant with James and John.*

42 *Calling them to Himself, Jesus said to them, "You know that those who are recognized as rulers of the Gentiles lord it over them; and their great men exercise authority over them.*

43 *"But it is not this way among you, but whoever wishes to become great among you shall be your servant;*

44 *and whoever wishes to be first among you shall be slave of all.*

45 *"For even the Son of Man did not come to be served, but to serve, and to give His life a ransom for many."*

DISCUSS with your GROUP or PONDER on your own . . .

What do James and John want from Jesus? How does this sit with the other disciples?

How do power-seekers sit with you? Have you ever considered how you affect the hearts of others when *you're* fishing for power? Explain.

How does Jesus contrast the world system with life in His kingdom? How do earthly rulers behave? Who will be great in Jesus' kingdom?

How is Jesus setting the example for this? What did He do to serve?

How does this sit with you? Are you getting used to "decreasing"? Explain.

@THE END OF THE DAY . . .

I don't know about you, but the application of these texts has been hitting me to the core. Let's spend some time praying and asking the Lord to reveal any pride that lingers in our hearts and to give us His power to follow Him in lives that seek the downward mobility of servanthood.

Week Five
Having the Attitude of Christ

Being found in appearance as a man, He humbled Himself
by becoming obedient to the point of death,
even death on a cross.
–Paul, Philippians 2:8

He did not come to be served. He came to serve. Not only this, Jesus also came to die—and not on behalf of good people. Jesus died for rebels, taking on our humanity for all eternity. The second person of the Trinity, the eternal Son of God chose to become the Son of Man in order to save. Along the way, He chose a humble life of submission to His parents, to His Father in heaven, and to a ministry that afforded him "nowhere to lay his head." "He was despised and forsaken of men, a man of sorrows and acquainted with grief" according to Isaiah 53:3. Jesus became one of us, dwelt among us, felt our pain, healed our diseases, and even washed feet like a common house servant. And in the end, He humbled Himself to the point of death to save us.

FYI:

Nowhere to Lay His Head
And Jesus said to him, "The foxes have holes and the birds of the air have nests, but the Son of Man has nowhere to lay His head."

–Luke 9:58

REMEMBERING

Take a few minutes to jot down how God has been changing the way you think and act as you've been studying His Word.

ONE STEP FURTHER:

Word Study: *phroneo*
In Philippians 2, the Greek verb *phroneo* appears three times. See if you can locate the occurrences and identify where else and how else the word is used throughout the New Testament. Record your findings below.

OBSERVE the TEXT of SCRIPTURE

We know from Philippians 1 that Paul is writing from prison and considers it a privilege to suffer for Christ's sake.

READ Philippians 2:1-11 and **MARK** *humility* and *humble*. **UNDERLINE** instances of humility in action.

Philippians 2:1-11

1   *Therefore if there is any encouragement in Christ, if there is any consolation of love, if there is any fellowship of the Spirit, if any affection and compassion,*

2   *make my joy complete by being of the same mind, maintaining the same love, united in spirit, intent on one purpose.*

3   *Do nothing from selfishness or empty conceit, but with humility of mind regard one another as more important than yourselves;*

4   *do not merely look out for your own personal interests, but also for the interests of others.*

5   *Have this attitude in yourselves which was also in Christ Jesus,*

6   *who, although He existed in the form of God, did not regard equality with God a thing to be grasped,*

7   *but emptied Himself, taking the form of a bond-servant, and being made in the likeness of men.*

8   *Being found in appearance as a man, He humbled Himself by becoming obedient to the point of death, even death on a cross.*

9   *For this reason also, God highly exalted Him, and bestowed on Him the name which is above every name,*

10   *so that at the name of Jesus EVERY KNEE WILL BOW, of those who are in heaven and on earth and under the earth,*

11   *and that every tongue will confess that Jesus Christ is Lord, to the glory of God the Father.*

ONE STEP FURTHER:

Word Study: selfishness
If you have time this week, find the Greek word translated *selfishness* in Philippians 2:3. Then see where else it is used throughout the New Testament. How else is it translated? What can we learn about the situations it describes? Record your findings below.

DISCUSS with your GROUP or PONDER on your own . . .

What does Paul assume about his audience? What are some of the traits he thinks already mark them?

What will make his joy full?

FYI:

Empty Conceit
In Philippians 2:3, the phrase "empty conceit" translates the Greek *kenodoxia* (literally "empty [*kenos*] glory [*doxa*]"). It is a rich word particularly in this context of Jesus emptying (*kenoo*) Himself on behalf of sinners to the ultimate glory (*doxa*) of God.

What motives does Paul tells his reader to avoid? Are these temptations in your life? If so, in what ways?

How does Paul describe humility of mind? What are some ways you can apply this? Try to answer with specifics.

How did Jesus model humility of mind? What did it cause Him to do and to avoid?

Specifically how did Jesus humble Himself according to verse 8?

Are you aware of any obedience problems in your life? If so, what?

ONE STEP FURTHER:

Garden of Gethsemane

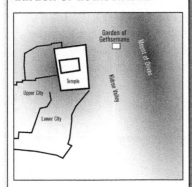

Both Matthew and Mark refer to Gethsemane in their accounts of Jesus' agonizing prayer prior to His betrayal by Judas and subsequent arrest. Both have Jesus going "out to the Mount of Olives" (Matthew 26:30, Mark 14:26) and coming to "a place named/called Gethsemane" (Matthew 26:36, Mark 14:32). In Aramaic Gethsemane literally means "oil press." While Luke (22:39) does not mention Gethsemane by name, he writes about the events taking place on the Mount of Olives and John (18:1) specifies that they take place "over the ravine of the Kidron, where there was a garden." In the map above, you can see Gethsemane's location in relation to the temple and the Kidron Valley.

OBSERVE the TEXT of SCRIPTURE

Being "obedient to the point of death" was not a slam dunk just because Jesus was God. Before going to the cross, Jesus wrestles in prayer in the Garden of Gethsemane.

READ Mark 14:32-42 and **MARK** every reference to *Jesus* including pronouns. Also **MARK** every reference to *prayer*.

Mark 14:32-42

32 *They came to a place named Gethsemane; and He said to His disciples, "Sit here until I have prayed."*

33 *And He took with Him Peter and James and John, and began to be very distressed and troubled.*

34 *And He said to them, "My soul is deeply grieved to the point of death; remain here and keep watch."*

35 *And He went a little beyond them, and fell to the ground and began to pray that if it were possible, the hour might pass Him by.*

36 *And He was saying, "Abba! Father! All things are possible for You; remove this cup from Me; yet not what I will, but what You will."*

37 *And He came and found them sleeping, and said to Peter, "Simon, are you asleep? Could you not keep watch for one hour?*

38 *"Keep watching and praying that you may not come into temptation; the spirit is willing, but the flesh is weak."*

39 *Again He went away and prayed, saying the same words.*

40 *And again He came and found them sleeping, for their eyes were very heavy; and they did not know what to answer Him.*

41 *And He came the third time, and said to them, "Are you still sleeping and resting? It is enough; the hour has come; behold, the Son of Man is being betrayed into the hands of sinners.*

42 *"Get up, let us be going; behold, the one who betrays Me is at hand!"*

DISCUSS with your GROUP or PONDER on your own . . .

Where does the scene take place? Who is with Jesus? What does He tell them to do?

What does Jesus tell the disciples *He* is going to do? What does He tell them about His soul's condition? What does Jesus' condition say about the gravity of the situation?

What does Jesus pray for? How many times does He ask?

What light does this passage shed on the statement in Philippians 2 that Jesus humbled Himself by becoming obedient to death? What toll did it take on Him?

Does understanding Jesus' struggle help you in your struggle to obey? If so, how?

What does Jesus say about the spirit and the flesh in verse 38? What does watching and praying have to do with these?

OBSERVE the TEXT of SCRIPTURE

On the heels of feeding the 5,000 and hearing Peter declare Him to be "the Christ of God," Jesus tells the disciples that He will suffer, "be killed, and be raised up on the third day" (Luke 9:22).

READ Luke 9:23-27 and **MARK** every reference to Jesus' hearers.

Luke 9:23-27

23   *And He was saying to* them *all, "If anyone wishes to come after Me, he must deny himself, and take up his cross daily and follow Me.*

24   *"For whoever wishes to save his life will lose it, but whoever loses his life for My sake, he is the one who will save it.*

25   *"For what is a man profited if he gains the whole world, and loses or forfeits himself?*

26   *"For whoever is ashamed of Me and My words, the Son of Man will be ashamed of him when He comes in His glory, and* the *glory of the Father and of the holy angels.*

27   *"But I say to you truthfully, there are some of those standing here who will not taste death until they see the kingdom of God."*

DISCUSS with your GROUP or PONDER on your own . . .

According to Jesus what is involved in coming after Him? Are these commands optional? Explain.

What did this involve for Jesus' disciples then? What does it mean for Jesus' disciples now?

How often are disciples called to take up the cross? What implications does this have?

According to the text, what are the challenges to following Jesus and how can we combat them?

Which of the challenges that Jesus mentions resonates most with you? In what way?

What are the temptations to shame associated with Jesus and His words? Are you progressing or regressing in this area? Explain.

How does Jesus' teaching compare with the world's typical way of thinking and living?

FYI:

Upside-Down Leadership

Public foot washing rarely enters the daily lives of those living in lands of shoes and showers. In ancient Israel and Judah, though, where sandals and dirt abounded, foot washing was part of life and normal hospitality included providing guests with water to wash their feet. In well-to-do Jewish homes, Gentile slaves washed feet as even Hebrew slaves were considered above that kind of work. Jesus again flips the cultural paradigm upside down as He humbles Himself to wash His disciples' feet and calls them to follow His example. Leadership never looked the same!

OBSERVE the TEXT of SCRIPTURE

READ John 13:1-17 and **MARK** references to *Jesus* including pronouns.

John 13:1-17

1 *Now before the Feast of the Passover, Jesus knowing that His hour had come that He would depart out of this world to the Father, having loved His own who were in the world, He loved them to the end.*

2 *During supper, the devil having already put into the heart of Judas Iscariot, the son of Simon, to betray Him,*

3 *Jesus, knowing that the Father had given all things into His hands, and that He had come forth from God and was going back to God,*

4 *got up from supper, and laid aside His garments; and taking a towel, He girded Himself.*

5 *Then He poured water into the basin, and began to wash the disciples' feet and to wipe them with the towel with which He was girded.*

6 So He came to Simon Peter. He said to Him, "Lord, do You wash my feet?"

7 Jesus answered and said to him, "What I do you do not realize now, but you will understand hereafter."

8 Peter said to Him, "Never shall You wash my feet!" Jesus answered him, "If I do not wash you, you have no part with Me."

9 Simon Peter said to Him, "Lord, then wash not only my feet, but also my hands and my head."

10 Jesus said to him, "He who has bathed needs only to wash his feet, but is completely clean; and you are clean, but not all of you."

11 For He knew the one who was betraying Him; for this reason He said, "Not all of you are clean."

12 So when He had washed their feet, and taken His garments and reclined at the table again, He said to them, "Do you know what I have done to you?

13 "You call Me Teacher and Lord; and you are right, for so I am.

14 "If I then, the Lord and the Teacher, washed your feet, you also ought to wash one another's feet.

15 "For I gave you an example that you also should do as I did to you.

16 "Truly, truly, I say to you, a slave is not greater than his master, nor is one who is sent greater than the one who sent him.

17 "If you know these things, you are blessed

ONE STEP FURTHER:

Other Foot Washers
If you have some extra time this week, see what you can discover about foot washing elsewhere in the Bible. *Where do you see it practiced? Who does it? etc.* Use a concordance to help you search and then record your findings below.

DISCUSS with your GROUP or PONDER on your own . . .

Describe the setting.

Looking specifically at verses 1-3, what does the text say that Jesus knew? In light of this, what does He do for His disciples?

How does Simon Peter react? Why?

What example is Jesus setting for His disciples then and now? How is it consistent with what He has been teaching and with what He is about to do?

What does He specifically tell the disciples to do in response to what they have seen? What is the inherent challenge in this to a disciple's ego, then and now?

Can you recall a time when someone else "washed your feet"? What effect did it have on you? How did you respond? Explain.

What are some ways disciples today can humble themselves to serve others? Is God bringing any particular "feet" into your mind? Just asking . . .

If we don't follow Jesus' example, what are we saying about ourselves in comparison to Him? Explain.

Digging Deeper

How Did Jesus Treat People?

Philippians 2 tells us about the attitude Jesus had and John 13 gives us a snapshot of that humility in action, but God has given us so much more truth about Jesus' life and actions in the Gospel accounts. If you have some extra time this week, invest some of it in reading (or listening) through the Gospels. If you have lots of time, read them all! If you're really short on time, try to read a portion of one of the Gospels to watch how Jesus treats real people in real life situations. Consider what you can learn from His example and record your findings below. As you read, you may want to look for patterns: *How does Jesus deal with repentant sinners? How does He deal with hardened religious types? How does He talk to Jews? How does He interact with Gentiles? Etc.*

Matthew

Mark

Luke

John

What did you learn from Jesus' example that will help you treat others more like He did?

OBSERVE the TEXT of SCRIPTURE

READ Galatians 5:16-26 and **MARK** every reference to the *Spirit* and the *flesh*.

Galatians 5:16-26

16 *But I say, walk by the Spirit, and you will not carry out the desire of the flesh.*

17 *For the flesh sets its desire against the Spirit, and the Spirit against the flesh; for these are in opposition to one another, so that you may not do the things that you please.*

18 *But if you are led by the Spirit, you are not under the Law.*

19 *Now the deeds of the flesh are evident, which are: immorality, impurity, sensuality,*

20 *idolatry, sorcery, enmities, strife, jealousy, outbursts of anger, disputes, dissensions, factions,*

21 *envying, drunkenness, carousing, and things like these, of which I forewarn you, just as I have forewarned you, that those who practice such things will not inherit the kingdom of God.*

22 *But the fruit of the Spirit is love, joy, peace, patience, kindness, goodness, faithfulness,*

23 *gentleness, self-control; against such things there is no law.*

24 *Now those who belong to Christ Jesus have crucified the flesh with its passions and desires.*

25 *If we live by the Spirit, let us also walk by the Spirit.*

26 *Let us not become boastful, challenging one another, envying one another.*

DISCUSS with your GROUP or PONDER on your own . . .

Describe life according to the flesh. What does it do? What is its disposition toward the Spirit?

Which "deeds of the flesh" are associated with selfishness and how are they related? Explain your answer.

ONE STEP FURTHER:

Romans 8
Along with Galatians 5 that we've already looked at this week, Romans 8 is *the* go-to passage in the New Testament for instruction on life in the Spirit. If you have some extra time this week, check out Romans 8 and list everything you learn about "those who are being led by the Spirit" (Romans 8:14).

Week Five: **Having the Attitude of Christ**

Describe a life that walks "by the Spirit." What does it exhibit?

How do those who live by the Spirit go about walking by the Spirit? What is the engine behind this behavior?

What passions and desires have been crucified in your life? Are there some areas where you are taking up your cross daily? Explain.

What is Paul's final instruction in this section? What dangers does he warn about with regard to "one another"?

How are you doing with the "one another"s in your life? Does undue competition and boasting or envy ever characterize you? If so, how did it slide in? If not, how are you keeping it at bay as you walk by the Spirit?

OBSERVE the TEXT of SCRIPTURE

READ Galatians 2:20 and **MARK** every reference to *live/life*

Galatians 2:20

20 *"I have been crucified with Christ; and it is no longer I who live, but Christ lives in me; and the life which I now live in the flesh I live by faith in the Son of God, who loved me and gave Himself up for me.*

DISCUSS with your GROUP or PONDER on your own . . .

How has Christ's obedience to the Father affected Paul? What happened to Paul when he was crucified with Christ?

Based on what you know about Paul's life, what kind of change occurred? (If you don't know much about Paul, skip this question or do the sidebar to learn some more!)

Since all believers, like Paul, have been crucified with Christ, what results should we see in their lives?

Where does the power to live a godly life come from? Explain.

Are you living in the light of this truth—in the power of the indwelling Spirit acknowledging your weakness and inability apart from Him? Explain.

ONE STEP FURTHER:

Pre-Conversion Paul

While Paul eventually wrote a large portion of what we now call the New Testament—the Church recognizing his letters to churches and to Timothy and Titus as God-breathed Holy Scripture—and ended up beheaded, martyred for the cause of Christ, nothing in his early life suggested that he would leave Pharisaic Judaism for anything! God's plans for Paul's life differed from Paul's plans. If you have time this week, look into Paul's backstory for yourself using the passages listed below as a starting point and recording what you learn as you go.

Saul (as he is referred to prior to his conversion and occasionally post-conversion) first appears on the biblical landscape in Acts 7:58 at the stoning of Stephen. After his conversion to Christ, he lives faithfully until his death at the hands of Rome shortly after writing his second letter to Timothy.

Acts 7:54–8:3

Acts 9:1–31

Galatians 1:11–24

Philippians 3:1–14

Digging Deeper

"Humility" for Show

One common way people expressed humility before God during biblical times was by fasting. While some fasted as an expression of truly repentant hearts, others made it into a show. If you have some extra time this week, see what you can discover from Scripture about those who truly humbled themselves before God as opposed to those who feigned humility. One passage you'll want to address is Isaiah 58 where God rejects Israel's fasts and tells them what He wants instead. Think through Scripture and be sure to use your concordance to help you with your search.

Examples of True Repentance/Humility:

Examples of False Humility:

Lessons from Isaiah 58:

Summarize your findings in a concise sentence or two focusing on practical application you've learned from your study time.

@THE END OF THE DAY . . .

Take a few moments to reflect on what you've learned this week and to consider Hebrews 12:1-3. Then jot down anything you need to remember.

> *Therefore, since we have so great a cloud of witnesses surrounding us, let us also lay aside every encumbrance and the sin which so easily entangles us, and let us run with endurance the race that is set before us, fixing our eyes on Jesus, the author and perfecter of faith, who for the joy set before Him endured the cross, despising the shame, and has sat down at the right hand of the throne of God. For consider Him who has endured such hostility by sinners against Himself, so that you will not grow weary and lose heart.*

—Hebrews 12:1-3

Week Six
Fools for Christ

. . . we preach Christ crucified, to Jews a stumbling block and to Gentiles foolishness, but to those who are the called, both Jews and Greeks, Christ the power of God and the wisdom of God.
–Paul, 1 Corinthians 1:23-24

In a world where image is everything, it's hard to be a fool for Christ. Christ calls His followers not only to take up a cross—in its day the most shameful way to die—but also to witness, to bring the word of the cross to the world and make disciples. His command is fully reasonable viewed from the perspective of eternity. Sometimes, though, when we're already neck-deep in the troubles of "today" the thought of following a Master who was "despised and forsaken of men" can be overwhelming. It's one thing to live in humble obedience, not puffing up but not rocking the boat either. It's another all together to live a sacrificial life that selflessly accepts mocking and rejection for being an ambassador for Christ.

Week Six: **Fools for Christ**

REMEMBERING

Review can seem so cumbersome, but it is critical to remembering and synthesizing what we've learned. So take some time to prayerfully look back through your Workbook and record the biggest lessons that God has been teaching you through His Word week by week. For each takeaway, record the verse of Scripture where your application came from.

WEEK 1

WEEK 2

WEEK 3

WEEK 4

WEEK 5

OBSERVE the TEXT of SCRIPTURE

READ Matthew 28:16-20 and **UNDERLINE** what Jesus commands His disciples to do.

Matthew 28:16-20

16 *But the eleven disciples proceeded to Galilee, to the mountain which Jesus had designated.*

17 *When they saw Him, they worshiped Him; but some were doubtful.*

18 *And Jesus came up and spoke to them, saying, "All authority has been given to Me in heaven and on earth.*

19 *"Go therefore and make disciples of all the nations, baptizing them in the name of the Father and the Son and the Holy Spirit,*

20 *teaching them to observe all that I commanded you; and lo, I am with you always, even to the end of the age."*

DISCUSS with your GROUP or PONDER on your own . . .

Who is Jesus talking to? Where are they? What has happened by this time?

What does Jesus tell them to do? On the basis of what authority?

How does this command apply to believers today?

How are you doing at obeying it? Explain.

INDUCTIVE FOCUS:

When Grammar Matters

Most of the time, good English Bible translations are clear. Occasionally, though, we do lose something in translation. However, with the abundance of study tools available today, anyone who chooses to make the effort can access information that not long ago was limited to Greek and Hebrew scholars.

One such piece of information is the mood of Greek verbs which differentiates between simple facts, commands, and probabilities. Looking at Matthew 28:19 the English reader sees two simple commands: "go" and "make disciples." When we take time to look at the Greek, we see that the mood of command (the imperative) is only present in the word "make disciples" (*matheteusate*), making it the key element of the verse. Wherever you are—on a foreign mission field or in your own backyard—Jesus' command is the same: make disciples!

79

OBSERVE the TEXT of SCRIPTURE

READ 1 Corinthians 1:18-31 and **MARK** *foolishness* and *wisdom*. Then read it one more time and **MARK** every reference to *God*.

1 Corinthians 1:18-31

18 *For the word of the cross is foolishness to those who are perishing, but to us who are being saved it is the power of God.*

19 *For it is written,*

   "I WILL DESTROY THE WISDOM OF THE WISE,

   AND THE CLEVERNESS OF THE CLEVER I WILL SET ASIDE."

20 *Where is the wise man? Where is the scribe? Where is the debater of this age? Has not God made foolish the wisdom of the world?*

21 *For since in the wisdom of God the world through its wisdom did not come to know God, God was well-pleased through the foolishness of the message preached to save those who believe.*

22 *For indeed Jews ask for signs and Greeks search for wisdom;*

23 *but we preach Christ crucified, to Jews a stumbling block and to Gentiles foolishness,*

24 *but to those who are the called, both Jews and Greeks, Christ the power of God and the wisdom of God.*

25 *Because the foolishness of God is wiser than men, and the weakness of God is stronger than men.*

26 *For consider your calling, brethren, that there were not many wise according to the flesh, not many mighty, not many noble;*

27 *but God has chosen the foolish things of the world to shame the wise, and God has chosen the weak things of the world to shame the things which are strong,*

28 *and the base things of the world and the despised God has chosen, the things that are not, so that He may nullify the things that are,*

29 *so that no man may boast before God.*

30 *But by His doing you are in Christ Jesus, who became to us wisdom from God, and righteousness and sanctification, and redemption,*

31 *so that, just as it is written, "LET HIM WHO BOASTS, BOAST IN THE LORD."*

DISCUSS with your GROUP or PONDER on your own . . .

Using your markings of *wisdom* and *foolishness* to help you, make a list that compares those who are perishing with those who are being saved.

ONE STEP FURTHER:

The Word of the Cross

Take some time to write down how you would describe the word of the cross to a friend who asked you about your beliefs. What elements are needed to clearly present the Gospel? Use appropriate Scripture as you write your explanation below.

Notes

Those who are perishing | **Those who are being saved**

Take a moment to briefly summarize what you recorded in your list above. How do the perishing compare with those who are being saved?

What does the text teach us about God and His wisdom?

Week Six: **Fools for Christ**

How has God chosen to save people? How does this compare with what people naturally crave?

How is the "word of the cross" perceived by many people? How then will its messengers look in their eyes? How will you look to unbelievers?

What types of things make you feel foolish? Why?

How is *appearing* foolish different from *being* foolish?

What Scriptures can help us overcome the fear of being thought a fool? Explain.

OBSERVE the TEXT of SCRIPTURE

READ 1 Corinthians 2:14, 3:18-23 and **MARK** *wise* and *foolish* and any synonyms.

1 Corinthians 2:14

14 But a natural man does not accept the things of the Spirit of God, for they are foolishness to him; and he cannot understand them, because they are spiritually appraised.

1 Corinthians 3:18-23

18 Let no man deceive himself. If any man among you thinks that he is wise in this age, he must become foolish, so that he may become wise.

19 For the wisdom of this world is foolishness before God. For it is written, "He is THE ONE WHO CATCHES THE WISE IN THEIR CRAFTINESS";

20 and again, "THE LORD KNOWS THE REASONINGS of the wise, THAT THEY ARE USELESS."

21 So then let no one boast in men. For all things belong to you,

22 whether Paul or Apollos or Cephas or the world or life or death or things present or things to come; all things belong to you,

23 and you belong to Christ; and Christ belongs to God.

FYI:

Be Encouraged!
While Satan blinds eyes, God opens them! *God*, not you. What a relief! Christians are never called to be saviors, only to be witnesses to the One who saves!

DISCUSS with your GROUP or PONDER on your own . . .

According to 1 Corinthians 2:14, what does the natural man think about "the things of the Spirit of God"? Why?

Given this, what is the only way a person can understand the Gospel? What kind of position does that put a witness in? (Weak/strong; dependent/independent; etc.)

Are you ready to be viewed as foolish by some people? If not, why not? If so, how have you come to accept this?

What two commands does Paul give in 1 Corinthians 3:18-23?

How are people inclined to deceive themselves? How can they truly become wise?

How does worldly wisdom show itself in your life? How do you identify it? How do you combat it?

What will worldly wisdom reap? Why?

According to Paul, what should we not boast in? Why?

Notes

Digging Deeper

Gratefulness and Pride

If you have some extra time this week, explore how thankfulness and a grateful heart counteract pride. Here are some verses to get you started: 1 Thessalonians 5:18, Philippians 4:4-7.

ONE STEP FURTHER:

Isaiah 53 and Jesus

If you have some extra time this week, compare Isaiah 53 with the Gospel accounts of Jesus' life and death. Note specific verses in the New Testament that fulfill the prophecies of Isaiah 53. Use the space below to summarize your findings or an extra sheet of paper if you need more room.

OBSERVE the TEXT of SCRIPTURE

READ Isaiah 53 and **MARK** every reference to the main subject, the *man of sorrows.*

Isaiah 53

1   *Who has believed our message? And to whom has the arm of the LORD been revealed?*

2   *For He grew up before Him like a tender shoot, And like a root out of parched ground; He has no stately form or majesty That we should look upon Him, Nor appearance that we should be attracted to Him.*

3   *He was despised and forsaken of men, A man of sorrows and acquainted with grief; And like one from whom men hide their face He was despised, and we did not esteem Him.*

4   *Surely our griefs He Himself bore, And our sorrows He carried; Yet we ourselves esteemed Him stricken, Smitten of God, and afflicted.*

5   *But He was pierced through for our transgressions, He was crushed for our iniquities; The chastening for our well-being fell upon Him, And by His scourging we are healed.*

6   *All of us like sheep have gone astray, Each of us has turned to his own way; But the LORD has caused the iniquity of us all To fall on Him.*

7 He was oppressed and He was afflicted, Yet He did not open His mouth; Like a lamb that is led to slaughter, And like a sheep that is silent before its shearers, So He did not open His mouth.

8 By oppression and judgment He was taken away; And as for His generation, who considered That He was cut off out of the land of the living For the transgression of my people, to whom the stroke was due?

9 His grave was assigned with wicked men, Yet He was with a rich man in His death, Because He had done no violence, Nor was there any deceit in His mouth.

10 But the LORD was pleased To crush Him, putting Him to grief; If He would render Himself as a guilt offering, He will see His offspring, He will prolong His days, And the good pleasure of the LORD will prosper in His hand.

11 As a result of the anguish of His soul, He will see it and be satisfied; By His knowledge the Righteous One, My Servant, will justify the many, As He will bear their iniquities.

12 Therefore, I will allot Him a portion with the great, And He will divide the booty with the strong; Because He poured out Himself to death, And was numbered with the transgressors; Yet He Himself bore the sin of many, And interceded for the transgressors.

DISCUSS with your GROUP or PONDER on your own . . .

Describe the Servant. What happened to Him and why?

How did people view and treat Him?

Since a servant is not greater than his Master, consider how you would feel if you were

• despised

• forsaken

• oppressed

• afflicted

Have you been subjected to any of these abuses? How did you respond (or are you responding)?

How does your response to suffering reflect on your Master?

OBSERVE the TEXT of SCRIPTURE

READ Matthew 10:24-25, John 13:1-17, and John 15:20 and **MARK** *slave, master* and *Lord.*

Matthew 10:24-25

24 *"A disciple is not above his teacher, nor a slave above his master.*

25 *"It is enough for the disciple that he become like his teacher, and the slave like his master. If they have called the head of the house Beelzebul, how much more will they malign the members of his household!*

Week Six: **Fools for Christ**

DISCUSS with your GROUP or PONDER on your own . . .

What two relationships does Matthew describe? How are they similar?

FYI:

Blessed are you when . . .

"Blessed are you when people insult you and persecute you, and falsely say all kinds of evil against you because of Me.

"Rejoice and be glad, for your reward in heaven is great; for in the same way they persecuted the prophets who were before you."

–Jesus, Matthew 5:11-12

How do these relate to everything we've been learning about Jesus? How do we fit in?

What does Jesus tell His disciples to expect from an unbelieving world? What can we learn from His example about how to deal with this world? Be specific.

OBSERVE the TEXT of SCRIPTURE

READ John 15:18-22 and also **MARK** *world* and *hates*.

John 15:18-22

18 *"If the world hates you, you know that it has hated Me before it hated you.*

19 *"If you were of the world, the world would love its own; but because you are not of the world, but I chose you out of the world, because of this the world hates you.*

20 *"Remember the word that I said to you, 'A slave is not greater than his master.' If they persecuted Me, they will also persecute you; if they kept My word, they will keep yours also.*

21 *"But all these things they will do to you for My name's sake, because they do not know the One who sent Me.*

22 *"If I had not come and spoken to them, they would not have sin, but now they have no excuse for their sin.*

DISCUSS with your GROUP or PONDER on your own . . .

Summarize Jesus' teaching about slaves and masters.

How did the world respond to Jesus? What did this mean for His disciples? How can knowing this fortify us to follow better?

What, if any, is the silver lining in being hated by the world?

@THE END OF THE DAY . . .

In a self-centered world of style and slick, are you willing to be a fool for Christ, a witness to what God has done in your life, and a servant of Christ and His Kingdom? As we close our study, take a little more time to prayerfully reflect on what you've learned from God's Word over the last several weeks. Then write down how you are applying and living the truth that you've learned. What changes have you been making? What changes is God continuing to make in your life as you follow Him fully?

Notes

RESOURCES

Helpful Study Tools

The New How to Study Your Bible
Eugene, Oregon: Harvest House
Publishers

The New Inductive Study Bible
Eugene, Oregon: Harvest House
Publishers

Logos Bible Software
Available at www.logos.com.

Greek Word Study Tools

Kittel, G., Friedrich, G., & Bromiley,
G.W.
*Theological Dictionary of the New
Testament, Abridged* (also known as
Little Kittel)
Grand Rapids, Michigan: W.B.
Eerdmans Publishing Company

Zodhiates, Spiros
*The Complete Word Study Dictionary:
New Testament*
Chattanooga, Tennessee: AMG
Publishers

Hebrew Word Study Tools

Harris, R.L., Archer, G.L., & Walker,
B.K.
*Theological Wordbook of the Old
Testament* (also known as TWOT)
Chicago, Illinois: Moody Press

Zodhiates, Spiros
*The Complete Word Study Dictionary:
Old Testament*
Chattanooga, Tennessee: AMG
Publishers

General Word Study Tools

Strong, James
*The New Strong's Exhaustive
Concordance of the Bible*
Nashville, Tennessee: Thomas Nelson

Recommended Commentary Sets

Expositor's Bible Commentary
Grand Rapids, Michigan: Zondervan

NIV Application Commentary
Grand Rapids, Michigan: Zondervan

The New American Commentary
Nashville, Tennessee: Broadman and
Holman Publishers

One-Volume Commentaries

Carson, D.A., France, R.T., Motyer,
J.A., & Wenham, G.J. Ed.
*New Bible Commentary: 21st Century
Edition*
Downers Grove, Illinois: Inter-Varsity
Press

Rydelnik, M.,.Vanlaningham, M., Ed.
The Moody Bible Commentary
Chicago, Illinois: Moody Publishers

HOW TO DO AN ONLINE WORD STUDY

For use with www.blueletterbible.org

1. Type in Bible verse. Change the version to NASB. Click the "Search" button.

2. When you arrive at the next screen, you will see a "Tools" button to left of your verse. Hover your mouse over the "Tools" button and select "Interlinear" (C) to bring up concordance information.

3. Click on the Strong's number which is the link to the original word in Greek or Hebrew.

Clicking this number will bring up another screen that will give you a brief definition of the word as well as list every occurrence of the Greek word in the New Testament or Hebrew word in the Old Testament. Before running to the dictionary definition, scan places where this word is used in Scripture and examine the general contexts where it is used.

ABOUT PRECEPT

Precept Ministries International was raised up by God for the sole purpose of establishing people in God's Word to produce reverence for Him. It serves as an arm of the church without respect to denomination. God has enabled Precept to reach across denominational lines without compromising the truths of His inerrant Word. We believe every word of the Bible was inspired and given to man as all that is necessary for him to become mature and thoroughly equipped for every good work of life. This ministry does not seek to impose its doctrines on others, but rather to direct people to the Master Himself, who leads and guides by His Spirit into all truth through a systematic study of His Word. The ministry produces a variety of Bible studies and holds conferences and intensive Training Workshops designed to establish attendees in the Word through Inductive Bible Study.

Jack Arthur and his wife, Kay, founded Precept Ministries in 1970. Kay and the ministry staff of writers produce **Precept Upon Precept** studies, **In & Out** studies, **Lord** series studies, the **New Inductive Study Series** studies, **40-Minute** studies, and **Discover 4 Yourself Inductive Bible Studies for Kids**. From years of diligent study and teaching experience, Kay and the staff have developed these unique, inductive courses that are now used in nearly 180 countries and 70 languages.

 PRECEPT.ORG

GET CONNECTED

LEARN HOW you can get involved in "Establishing People in God's Word" at precept.org/connect

Use your smartphone to connect to Precept's ministry initiatives.
Precept.org/connect

PRECEPT ONLINE COMMUNITY provides support, training opportunities and exclusive resources to help Bible study leaders and students. Connect at Precept Online Community at Precept.org/POC.

Use your smartphone to connect to Precept Online Community.
Precept.org/POC

PAM GILLASPIE

Pam Gillaspie, a passionate Bible student and teacher, authors Precept's *Sweeter Than Chocolate!*® and *Cookies on the Lower Shelf*™ Bible study series. Pam holds a BA in Biblical Studies from Wheaton College in Wheaton, Illinois. She and her husband live in suburban Chicago, Illinois with their son, daughter, and Great Dane. Her greatest joy is encouraging others to read God's Word widely and study it deeply . . . precept upon precept.

Connect with Pam at:

www.pamgillaspie.com

 pamgillaspie

 pamgillaspie